ANGELS WATCHING OVER ME

BETTY MALZ

Chosen Books

A Division of Baker Book House
Grand Rapids, Michigan 49506

Edited by Ann McMath
Designed by Ann Cherryman

Copyright © 1986 by Fleming H. Revell
Published by Chosen Books
a division of Baker Book House Company
P.O. Box 6287, Grand Rapids, Michigan 49516-6287

ISBN: 0-8007-9056-1

ISBN 1-56865-152-X

Printed in the United States of America

*This book is dedicated to bringing hope
to the helpless
and offering help
to the fearful*

CONTENTS

CONTENTS

ACKNOWLEDGMENTS

My appreciation to:
   Ann McMath for her editorial advice
   Len LeSourd who challenged me to take this
      assignment
   P.J. Zondervan who believed that I could do it
   My friend Vicky Hagen for her prayer support
and to:
   Dwight Fearing
   Delores Eggen
   Gloria Hutchens
   Sheri Knipe
   Dr. Donald Van Hoozier
   Veva Rose
   Dr. Marvin Perkins, my brother
   Clarinne Koeppe
   Carl Nelson
   Patty Opsal
   John Pryor and Mark Torness
   Rev. Millington from England
for their input, research, and suggestions.

INTRODUCTION

I once commented to our old missionary friend Morris Plotts, "I'd like to read a good book on working angels."

"Why don't you write one then?" he said simply.

"Not me," I protested. I was hesitant about tackling such a big subject, though angels held a fascination for me. Plus, my practical nature did not want me to be classified with people who mount angels on their automobiles for hood ornaments and boast of private angel-servants on command.

He pressed the point. "Read the 'future' book," he said, "the prophetic book of things to come, Revelation. It mentions angels all the way through, who in the last days will govern the affairs of men and nations, control the weather and war, fight battles, declare the Gospel of Jesus, and announce His coming back to the earth again. More and more," he added thoughtfully, "as we draw closer to that day, angels are helping God's servants reach the ends of the earth with the Gospel."

I agreed it all sounded like a fascinating study, and later I wondered if he was really right about angels' increased activity in this world. Mostly, it seems, we are not even aware of them, or else we remember them only as celestial beings who heralded important events in Bible times.

I tried to put the suggestion aside but, curiously, it seemed to pursue me, and I came to realize he *was* right. Whenever I traveled on a speaking tour, whether being interviewed before a nationwide television audience or talking with a fellow airline passenger, someone would excitedly confide his own angel story. My friend Morris was not without one, either, perhaps the most fascinating I have ever heard. Even television commercials seemed to jump out at me with the clever use of angel characters.

And I discovered that the more I pondered the angel book, the more I felt driven to write about the encouragement evident in their activities. I wanted to write a comforting book that would stimulate ordinary people to tap the extraordinary resources of angelic assistance. I became utterly convinced that God uses angels to help us through the impossible places of life, times we cannot make it unless He helps us.

This book, then, is a practical journey of adventure. It is not meant to entertain, but to search out the ways angels work, the specific times they help us, and how we can have the right perspective about them. Some of the stories will sound almost incredible, but then, no more so than biblical accounts of angels at work.

It was a fascinating search, one that actually began years ago with my own encounter with an angel—my guardian angel. Perhaps my story is not typical in that I am alive to tell about it, for amazingly enough, I had to die to begin to understand the significant role angels play in our lives.

But now I'm getting ahead of myself.

Swing low, sweet chariot,
Comin' for to carry me home.
Swing low, sweet chariot,
Comin' for to carry me home.
 All night, all day,
 Angels watchin' over me, my Lord.
 All night, all day,
 Angels watchin' over me.

   (From "Swing Low, Sweet Chariot")

1

BETWEEN TWO WORLDS

When we left for vacation that spring of 1959 I had no idea how my life was about to change. My husband, daughter, and I were traveling with my parents to sunny Florida, and other than a nagging uneasiness, which I chose to ignore, my life could not have been better.

I attributed my security to my very practical faith—I had given my heart to Jesus as a child and knew I would go to heaven when I died—and I felt satisfied at my refusal to believe anything I could not see or explain. Since there was no earthly reason for me to feel apprehensive, I continued to shrug off a slight discomfort in my side that tugged for attention.

Then, suddenly one night, I passed the stage of warning. I felt as though something was exploding in my side, boiling and burning mercilessly. An ambulance rushed me to a hospital near our hotel.

Doctors struggled for days with a diagnosis until surgery revealed that I had suffered a ruptured appendix eleven days before, and that a mass of gangrene had coated all of my organs, causing them to disintegrate. Even as I lapsed into a coma I argued with the likelihood of such news, while my praying family thanked God that I had lived as long as I had. Out of my hearing, the doctors explained to my family that further complications of pneumonia and collapsed veins meant I could not live long.

Early one morning, after I had hung on in a coma for forty-four days, the night nurse on the third floor came to check my vital signs and found no response to her probings. I had slipped from this life into the next. At five a.m. a doctor pronounced me clinically dead, pulled a sheet over my head, and left the room in darkness. That was the state in which my father, who had awakened in the night with an urgent desire to be with me, found me twenty-eight minutes later.

I knew nothing of these earthly activities, of course. I felt as though I were on a roller coaster ride at Disneyland, and arrived at my destination when I reached the highest peak of exhilaration. It was much like taking the fastest jet imaginable from earth to another planet—a bright and glorious place under a deep blue sky. There was no fear, only peacefulness and beauty.

I was immediately aware of majestic music, filled with exquisite harmonies from countless choirs. Around my feet living waves of flowers splashed the velvet green meadows with color.

I felt fulfilled, youthful, alive as I walked tall and erect up a beautiful hill toward a brilliant city. I had never experienced such joy or eager anticipation.

Then I realized I was not alone. I glanced to my left and saw a tall companion in flowing white robes. An angel! I remembered childhood thoughts about angels, wondering what they did and what they looked like, but I could never have imagined a being with such beauty, power, and assurance. His face had masculine features; his hands were large and strong.

I felt comfortable in his presence, and somehow knew that he had been with me from the time I was thirteen and asked Jesus to be my Lord and Savior. I had never known he was there, possibly because I had never been so aware of my surroundings—or my need. For, without a doubt, he was a necessary part of my transition from the life I was leaving to the new life just ahead.

Silently, side by side, we took long, even strides up the sloping hillside. We spoke no words, but communicated easily just by thinking what we wanted to express. I also realized we could travel as quickly as our thoughts could choose a destination. For instance, a desire to see my earthly grandmother of my childhood days could transport us to her porch swing with warm summer breezes and honeysuckle sweetening the air. Yet we walked steadily toward our mutual destination.

We reached an enormous sheet of translucent pearl, apparently a gate in the city walls, through which I could detect a great brightness. My guardian angel reached his hand out to touch it, and as if from the warmth of his touch, a hand-sized opening melted outward to the borders of the gate.

Instantly I was bathed in a warm light and felt completely whole. Every yearning of my heart found fulfillment in the flooding power of that light. Many times during shining moments of accomplishment in my life, there had remained a small cavity of emptiness in the secret chambers of my soul. I knew now that that had been the longing for this new home; nothing else could fill it.

My eyes were drawn to the One who sat on a golden throne, and I saw the source of the dazzling light. The face of Jesus glowed with a brilliance too bright to behold. I looked down. It reflected on the golden boulevard in the center of the city, and was the same light that flowed through me.

Others besides my companion and me were drawn by the power of that light. I recognized people around the throne who had died during my lifetime, and they knew me. We shared the knowledge that we had achieved our true identities, we had become what we had always yearned to be.

Many people were doing just what people do on earth, though without any hindrance or handicap. I watched as several florists busily tended some delicate flowers like the ones I had admired on the way up the hill. Yet here they were working for a different employer in a perfect setting—no drought, no bugs, no backaches. Likewise, builders were busy constructing dwellings (I knew somehow that they were expecting large numbers of people soon) and countless others pursued their dreams.

I thought I would never want to leave that awesome place, but that was to change. Looking to the right I watched as shafts of light, ascending directly from the earth, entered the throne room and the presence of the original great Light—the Source of all energy, warmth, creativity, and power. The shafts of light, straight and swift as laser beams, were prayers. And standing all around the throne room were armies of angels waiting for orders to execute the answers.

On a particular shaft, I saw as well as heard a one-word prayer, and I recognized the voice of the one praying. It was my father. He simply breathed the name *Jesus*, and in it was a wish that I had not died. His prayer became my desire.

Immediately I felt as though I were on a fast elevator, descending at an alarming speed. Then I slowed down and stopped. All was still. I opened my eyes in my hospital room and looked into my dad's astonished face. I had returned to life.

The doctor who had declared me dead was shocked. He validated that I had been dead for twenty-eight minutes, and sent me home two days later with no discernible physical difficulties from my extraordinary experience.

But I had learned invaluable lessons. I now have a better understanding of human relationships, for instance, and feel an overwhelming desire to tell others about Jesus. I also learned that I must not believe only what I can explain with my practical logic. And I realized that next to the ultimately fulfilling presence of God, what amazed me most were the activities of His ministering angels, beings I had never seen or bothered much about, although I had pleasant childhood associations with the idea of angels.

As early as I can remember, a painting entitled "Guardian Angel" hung in my grandparents' home. It showed a little boy and girl on a bridge that spanned a waterfall. The boy was picking wild flowers, leaning over several missing planks in the bridge, while his little sister was holding the flowers he had already picked. Perhaps they were picking them for a sick grandmother, or to surprise their parents at home. In any event, the message that came through to me at an early age was that the large angel behind them was assigned to protect them, especially since they were picking the flowers for someone else.

One night during a terrible storm I snuggled close to my grandmother and hid my face so I couldn't see the lightning and hear the deafening claps of thunder. Mom Burns reached for her flashlight, shone the beam on the guardian angel picture, and quoted Psalm 91:11. "For he shall give his angels charge over thee, to keep thee in all thy ways" (KJV).

Somehow the painting helped me picture what the Bible verse meant. The children were in a dangerous situation, but they were being "kept in all their ways." Thinking about God's angels protecting me, too, in a dangerous situation helped me not be afraid.

Twenty-two years later that lesson of angelic protection was driven home. My six-year-old daughter, Brenda, and I were home alone, praying for safety as a tornado destroyed dozens of houses around us. I pointed to the guardian angel picture, which now hung in our living room, and spoke aloud the verse from Psalm 91.

Within seconds, our house was hit by the force of the tornado. Winds lifted the roof with a tremendous crack. Brenda and I huddled close in the corner. When we could finally uncover our faces and look around us, we saw that only one wall was left standing, while the two of us and Smokey, our small dog, were safe without a scratch.

Two miles away from where our house had stood I found some family photos, a light fixture, and the water-soaked guardian angel picture. It now is a treasured reminder of God's protection through his ministering angels. I knew for certain they were around us, helping us.

As a matter of fact, it seems I have survived a number of life-threatening situations, so many that I always remember with a smile the way.I was introduced at a Full Gospel Business Men's Convention in San Angelo, Texas. A big Texan put his arm around my shoulder and said to the audience, "This is Betty Malz. With all she has survived, you might say this cat has nine lives!" Everyone laughed, and I have since mused inwardly that God must have needed an extra crew of guardian angels for me, a well-meaning but often unwise young woman:

I was stillborn at birth, took poison once by mistake thinking it was medicine, and nearly married a mentally deranged man because he was good-looking and because I was deceived by my lonely heart. I survived a ruptured appendix, managed to veer my car at the last second from a gaping sinkhole in Florida, and lived through the tornado that destroyed our home in Indiana. I escaped from an overturned car in North Dakota, and almost crashed in a plane over Santa Ana, California.

Now that I have walked side-by-side with my angel and have seen countless other angels standing by the throne ready for instruction, I not only believe that angels exist—I have become increasingly fascinated with their activity here on earth. I know they are commissioned on our behalf—I watched them bolt like lightning to fulfill God's commands—but I began to be intrigued by a succession of questions. Do I have just one guardian angel? Or are there other angels available to intervene on my behalf? Just when can we human beings look for their help? When do they oversee ordinary, day-to-day activities? Is my angel always watching over me, by my side at every moment? I thought I knew the answer to that last question. I believed he was always with me; yet there was something significant about his presence in that experience of walking through death that only led to more questions about angels' help in our lives.

Was there some common denominator in these and other experiences that might explain when angels are available to help?

In all of the stories of angels that I ran across I did find a common denominator—aside from their willingness to help: all the people angels assisted seemed to be caught in some kind of gap. By that I mean they had a need they were powerless to meet. Perhaps they lacked the strength or knowledge or physical stamina to change a situation. During my near-death experience, for instance, I was helped by an angel in a gap between two worlds.

Just as God sought someone in Old Testament times to "stand in the gap" for Israel through intercession (see Ezekiel 22:30), so we are sometimes called to stand in a gap, whether of intercession or action. The personal experiences I encountered fell into five specific gap situations. You may be as surprised as I was to find that we are in these gaps far more than we realize. What a comfort to know that the Lord's hosts are *always* watching over us!

2
WHEN DO ANGELS COME?

My minister father almost regretted opening our rural community's Wednesday prayer meeting one night with this question: "Does anyone have an answer to prayer you would like to tell us about before we take prayer requests?"

Several hands went up, and my father nodded to a man sitting in the row behind me. I was a child, but even to me Clyde seemed a frail little man, unlike his rotund wife Samantha. Standing, his hat in his hands, Clyde told us his story.

"I was tryin' to sleep last night, but there were a mouse in our closet that jest kep' gnawin' and makin' a racket. So I prayed and told God to send an angel to kill that pesky mouse fer me.

"Shore 'nuff," Clyde continued, "this mornin' right by the closet door, there it were. Flat as a pancake."

From the look of polite consternation on my father's face, I knew he must have been groping for a spiritual conclusion. Before he could think up one, Samantha, who was seated directly behind me, rolled forward and stood up. I knew from experience that whenever she sat behind me and rose to her feet, her enormous stomach would bounce my head forward. So I slid to the edge of my pew and turned to look at her with what I hoped, under my parents' watchful eyes, was respectful interest.

"Folks," she said with a big smile, "I cain't let this go by. That weren't no angel that killed that mouse. 'Twere me, myself. I took Clyde's house slipper and smashed it." She heaved herself down in her pew, whereupon Clyde popped up once more.

"That's okay," he said, nodding to the smiling faces turned up at him. "It jest goes to show that God can use any old thing to he'p His angels answer your prayin'."

My father had apparently collected his thoughts by that time, and responded good-naturedly, but I hardly heard, my attention was so captivated by Clyde's face. I'll never forget his satisfied look as he explained the wonders of God's angels as he saw them.

As I thought of that humorous episode years later, I agreed that God can indeed use "any old thing" to work out His plans for good, though perhaps we should be more selective in what jobs we expect angels to perform!

Somehow I doubted that angels would be dispatched for work we could easily handle ourselves, or for foolish fancy. But I wondered. . . . If there are certain times we know angels *won't* come, are there guaranteed times they *will* come? What kinds of distresses must we be facing before they will act on our behalf? If we knew more about their ministry, perhaps we could understand when to look for them. Just what was a proper understanding of the role of angels in our lives?

The Bible seemed the best place to find an answer. And even a quick look through my concordance left me amazed at the many accounts of angels in Scripture.

An angel helped Abraham's servant choose a wife for Isaac (Genesis 24:7).

Jacob saw angels ascending and descending a heavenly ladder as they received and delivered communications and executed God's desires for His children (Genesis 28:12).

Moses received instructions through the angel of the Lord in the burning bush (Exodus 3:2).

While Balaam was planning to curse the children of God for personal profit, there stood in the path before him, though he could not detect it, an angel of the Lord. The mule saw it, however, and would not trot past the angelic roadblock. This saved the lives of many Israelites, including Balaam himself (Numbers 22:32–33).

Angels announced not only Jesus' birth but also His resurrection (Luke 1–2; Matthew 28:5–7); and they will be with Jesus when He comes again (Matthew 24:30–31; 1 Thessalonians 4:16).

An angel visited Paul, giving him assurance that later saved 276 souls from shipwreck (Acts 27:22–24).

An angel visited the house of Cornelius at three o'clock one afternoon and told him that God had heard his many prayers and seen what he had done for the people. Because of this visit, Cornelius' household was saved (Acts 10:2–3).

An angel of the Lord directed Philip in his ministry (Acts 8:26–40).

Angels rejoice over sinners who repent (Luke 15:10) and are witnesses when Jesus declares us to be His followers (Luke 12:8).

As followers of Jesus—the King of Angels as a hymn declares—we look to Him as the supreme example of the Christian life. And from the number of accounts recorded in the Bible of Jesus' alliance with angels, I concluded they must be an important—even vital—part of God's dealings with His earthly children.

Almost everyone is familiar with the stories of angels surrounding Jesus' birth—how they brought the news to Mary, Joseph, the shepherds in the fields. But what about His life as an adult? What connection did He have then with angels?

In the Gospel of Matthew, Jesus first appeared publicly at His baptism in the Jordan River. Immediately afterward, we are told in chapter four, the Holy Spirit led Him into the wilderness where He fasted and was tempted by the devil. After He had rejected the devil's temptation, we read: "Then the devil left him, and angels came and attended him" (verse 11). Jesus needed strength for a spiritual battle against a relentless enemy. He was hungry and physically weak, and angels came and ministered to Him, giving Him just what He needed.

Suppose you and I have also been fighting spiritual battles, trying to change our world for the better. Should we expect angels to minister to us with supernatural power? That seems almost too good to be true!

Jesus lived a perfect life. He obeyed the Father in all things. It seems absolutely right that He should have heavenly assistance. But remember that He is our example. I cannot live a perfect life, but I can try to do my best to be like Him. First Peter 1:15 says that "just as he who called you is holy, so be holy in all you do." Could it be that my struggle to "grow up into him who is the Head" (Ephesians 4:15), to follow His example, includes an expectant belief, as He Himself had, in angelic help?

I couldn't help but wonder about other men and women of faith in the Bible, and I found almost invariably that God's servants were ministered to in difficult situations by angels.

When Elijah, for instance, went to Mount Carmel to prove to the Baal worshipers that there was only one true God, he was helpless to convince them on his own (see 1 Kings 18:21). Elijah had challenged fifty false prophets to a test. They would each prepare a sacrificial offering. Then the followers of Baal were to call on their god to send fire to consume their offering, and Elijah would pray to his

God to light the other. Whoever answered with fire from heaven would be acknowledged as the true God.

Elijah could not have brought fire down from the sky any more than the Baal worshipers could, but he trusted God to act. After the pagans' failure to light the offering, to further prove it was God at work, Elijah doused the slain bull and the wood around it with water three times.

Then he looked up to heaven and prayed: "O Lord, God of Abraham, Isaac and Israel, let it be known today that you are God in Israel and that I am your servant and have done all these things at your command. Answer me, O Lord, answer me, so these people will know that you, O Lord, are God, and that you are turning their hearts back again" (1 Kings 18:36–37).

I like to imagine scores of angels with fiery torches gathering at the gate of heaven, receiving the command, "Go!" The fire poured out of heaven.

When the offering was consumed with flames that licked up even the water in the surrounding trench, Elijah killed the fifty false prophets and won quite a few converts to the true God.

His experience of angelic assistance came not long after. When Elijah heard that the wicked Queen Jezebel intended to avenge the blood of her slain prophets on him, he fled into the wilderness and hid under a tree. Apparently fear had caused him to forget that when we are serving God, He keeps us in His protective care. After telling the Lord how weary and discouraged he was, he slept.

But Elijah had never moved out from under the Lord's protection. He had been obedient and the Lord did not forget him. An angel appeared with nourishment and jostled Elijah awake: "Arise, and eat." Elijah was fed cake and water in a parched and dry land, and went for forty days on the strength of that one heaven-sent meal.

This account of the Old Testament prophet gives us at least three important directives for expecting angelic assistance. First, *Be obedient.* If we enter an impossible situation through the Lord's leading, we can expect His hosts to defend us. Second, *Be selfless.* If we are promoting a self-serving cause we have no right to look for helpful divine intervention. But if we are doing what God calls us to do, out of a motive of love and service to others, we can and should expect special treatment. And third, *Honor God.* This may be the most important principle of all. Aren't we supposed to love the Lord God with all our heart, soul, mind, and strength?

About the time I was first absorbing these angelic lessons from Elijah, I was also preparing to speak at the Minneapolis Convention Center at a Lowell Lundstrom Ministries Camp Meeting. In the weeks before the convention, my husband and I had attended to our daughter's graduation, tried to sell our farm, packed and moved to North Dakota, and hosted a seven-day reunion with fifteen people in our new home. On top of that, I had had a root canal, an abscess, an infection in my bladder, and leg cramps.

On the July day I was to speak, the humidity in

Minnesota measured ninety-two percent. I was just about to cancel out—I could not endure it physically—when I recalled how angels had ministered to Jesus and Elijah. I remembered the words from Scripture, "Ye ask and receive not because ye ask amiss" (James 4:3, KJV). And I couldn't escape the conviction that He wanted me to speak at the Convention Center that night. So, I decided to ask Him for angelic help.

Hours later, exhausted but obedient, I stepped up to the podium, and certain words of the Apostle Paul's came to mind. I smiled and spoke a variation of them into the microphone: "I, Betty, come not to you with enticing words, but with a toothache, a leg ache, a bladder infection, and runs in my stockings."

We all laughed, and I felt new strength. I was there to help minister to the needs of people, and like Jesus, my example, I would pray for them.

Then, at the very moment I vowed inwardly to stand firm and believe that God would meet my needs in order for me to serve Him, I felt a pulsating sensation all over my body, even in my scalp. As the current-like force passed through me, the aches and pains left, and we enjoyed a glorious evening together.

Now, I can't report that I saw an angel doctor with a medical bag, or that everyone in the audience observed a glowing nimbus over my head. But I can say that Jesus sends provisions on the wings of angels, and that I am still going on the strength of that answered prayer. Like Elijah, I was exhausted until I tapped His energy. What joy I felt at Jesus' desire to send those throne-room angels here to help us.

My enthusiasm was almost short-circuited a few days later when a woman named LoRae came to me with a troubling question. She was a young mother whose twenty-eight-year-old husband, a pilot, had died in a plane crash. We talked about Bill's death, until this young widow's voice burst out angrily: "Where was Bill's guardian angel when he crashed into that bridge? My relatives are religious people and told me he is safe in the arms of Jesus because he was a believer. But that's not much comfort. My in-laws say it was predestined— what is to be will be and cannot be diverted—and they told me to change my bitterness to relinquishment. But that just leaves me with more questions. Why pray for safety? Why pray at all?"

When I didn't answer right away, LoRae repeated her unresolved question: "Why didn't an angel protect Bill?"

I could not think of a satisfying answer, but I could pray for one. So we bowed our heads and I prayed for her comfort, asking God to heal her grief. Then I asked God to speak to her personally. We are all the same distance, after all, from the throne room of God; we can all enter it by prayer. She seemed more peaceful after we prayed, and I hoped that soon we would both know the answer to her question.

Months later, I learned how LoRae's grief did lift. She married a fine young man whose wife had died from a heart condition. She found happiness. And in a telephone conversation one day, as LoRae reminisced about her first husband, I stumbled upon what seemed to be the answer to her question.

He had been nicknamed "Wild Bill" for the foolhardy chances he sometimes took while flying. He was most cautious in his business flights, or when his family flew with him, but when alone he seemed to revel in danger. He had been warned by the county sheriff that another infraction of the law, such as flying lower than the five-thousand-foot ceiling, would cost him his license. The day of the crash, two motorists had stopped to report to the police a pilot "buzzing" cars on the highway below, and diving over and under power lines. Bill even flew low and close enough to talk by radio with truckers on their CB's.

Suddenly all seemed clear. I had just been reading a variety of Scripture passages that had to do with God's caring love. They made it clear that no one can pluck us out of the hollow of His hand; that He keeps us as the apple of His eye; that He protects us under the shadow of His wing. In other words, He will never *dump* us out of the hollow of His hand, but we can carelessly *jump* out. Paul writes in the first few verses of Romans 13 that "everyone must submit to the governing authorities. Do what is right and he (the one in charge) will commend you. For he is God's servant to do you good."

LoRae finally saw as well as I did that it was possible to violate the laws of government, of nature, of any established authority, and move out of the "safety zone" in which angels will protect us. Bill's choice to break federal aviation laws removed him from the sphere of angelic protection. He put his survival in his own hands, and took one too many chances.

I do not feel that the perimeters of angelic protection are so fragile that we should fear making one false move and losing that help forever. But I do believe that, so long as man's laws accord with God's laws, He expects us to follow their conditions and limitations. Choosing to disobey them does block angelic assistance just as surely as unbelief limits God's work in our lives.

Does this mean we will have no hardships? I think not. Our church congregation used to sing these lines from an old hymn: "Must Jesus bear the cross alone and all the world go free? No, there's a cross for everyone, and there's a cross for me." We must be willing to go where Jesus leads us, for as He told His disciples, "If anyone would come after me, he must deny himself and take up his cross and follow me" (Matthew 16:24).

Paul spent a considerable amount of time in chains for preaching the Gospel, yet he was rescued and guided by angels as well. Peter must have remembered that Jesus told him, "Simon, Simon, Satan has asked to sift you as wheat. But I have prayed for you, Simon, that your faith may not fail. And when you have turned back, strengthen your brothers" (Luke 22:31–32). Did angels minister to Peter, fight on his behalf, and defend him until he turned, stronger than ever to serve his Lord? Did angels keep him in their care as he was tried sorely, until he was able to bear even death for his Lord? Yes!

Each of us may be called in turn to serve in different ways, but we know God will not let us be tempted beyond what we are able to bear (1 Corinthians 10:13). Our God is a good God who does not want us to suffer senseless tragedies.

But that thought may make us a little uneasy. As with Bill, it puts a certain responsibility on *us*. He is perfect and loving; He wants us to lay hold of His provisions. So why do we seem to fall so short of the mark? If we are trying to obey legitimate authority, live good, unselfish lives, and honor God, and if angels surround us, willing to protect us, then why do we so often find ourselves struggling helplessly?

Could it be that we fail to take advantage of our prerogative as believers to pray, actively pray, for angels to help us serve God?

After my conversation with LoRae, I thought of the verse that came to mind that hot July night at the convention when the Lord answered my prayer for strength: "Ye have not because ye ask not." I realized I had a lot to learn about this kind of praying, but the more I discovered stories of angels' appearances in answer to specific prayers, the more I felt assured this was indeed important.

One of these stories was relayed by a young father I met shortly before an appearance on a Christian television program.

Steve Doherty, who works for the Trinity Broadcasting Network, told me of the struggle he and his wife, Theresa, had once had getting their young son to sleep peacefully through the night. I was especially interested in this problem since I get letters and phone calls constantly from parents whose children between the ages of four and nine are afraid to go to sleep.

For two long years, every night from the time he was four, Ryan Doherty would cry at bedtime, beg to sleep with his parents, and wake up several times in the night terrified from nightmares. Steve and Theresa tried everything. They played Christian music, read happy bedtime stories, reassured him, prayed with him—even spanked him. They counseled with a pediatrician and talked with a children's psychiatrist; and always, it seemed, they were told that they had done everything they could to assure Ryan he was safe and loved. They were completely baffled.

Finally an elderly gentleman in their church suggested they try two things. First, he said, when Ryan went to bed, they should have him breathe the name *Jesus* until he fell asleep. Second, they should read aloud a certain prayer in Ryan's room after he fell asleep each night; he wrote a copy out for them. It spoke of faith in the Word of God, and the safety Ryan had surrounding him as a child of God.

Steve and Theresa had prayed similar prayers before, with the exception, they noticed, of one line: "We believe and confess that You will give Your angels charge over Ryan and accompany and defend and preserve him in all his ways."

That night they followed their friend's suggestions, and awoke the next morning astonished that they had not once been disturbed by calls from Ryan in the night. Soon their son burst into their bedroom, all smiles.

"Ryan, you slept all night long!" Steve told me he had exclaimed.

"I sure did, Dad," he replied. "I wasn't afraid after that angel came."

Steve and Theresa exchanged glances. "What angel, honey?" asked Theresa.

"The one who was here last night. Didn't you see him?"

They shook their heads.

"Oh. Well, he walked down the hall and stopped at your door and looked at you, and then he came into my room. He stood by my bed, and slid his hand under my head. And do you know what he said?"

Again they shook their heads.

"He said, 'Ryan, don't you ever be afraid again.'"

"What did he look like?" asked Steve.

"Like Jesus," he answered without hesitation. "He wore a dress and there was a light with him. It looked like the dining room curtains when the sun comes through. He lit up my room."

From that night on, Ryan has slept peacefully, secure in the assurances of his visitor, and Steve and Theresa believe that an angel ministered to their son's needs.

I have since learned of many children from a

variety of locations and backgrounds who have seen Jesus or an angel like Him. I have gathered stories of equal intensity from adults of all ages. And as I mentioned earlier, I discovered that the examples seem to fall under one of five gaps.

These are times in which we struggle between danger and safety; between direction and indecision; between helplessness and rescue; between temptation and strength; and between prayer and its fulfillment.

In each of these gaps, which we will study in the chapters that follow, I have learned over and over the truth of the slogan, "God pays all bills He authorizes." When we take chances on our own, in ministry or business or finances, we take a risk. But if God directs us to do something, He will provide the desire, the means, the tools, and the wherewithal. If necessary, He will even send a managing angel to help us through the gap.

3

PROTECTING
ANGELS

All my life I have heard stories of Christians who were protected miraculously or saved from some peril by mysterious, unseen force. When I could find no practical explanation, I began to observe the gap principle at work: While God's servants stand obediently in gaps they are powerless to fill, angels protect them. The first gap, between danger and safety, is distinct from the other gaps in that these individuals know they are walking into perilous situations, yet they do so out of obedience to God.

We probably have no idea how often we have been kept safe by angels. Maybe this is because we have a wrong perception of angels, imagining them as the greeting card variety of plump, dimpled cherubs. Though angels can apparently appear in many different forms, the Scriptures depict them as powerful, fearless soldiers who take care of us in dangerous situations.

When Louis Torres, who directs a Teen Challenge Center in Philadelphia, spoke to our church congregation one Sunday morning, he confirmed that biblical perception.

A young woman named Myra, working for Teen Challenge in that rough ghetto area, was concerned for the young people who had shown interest in receiving Christian counsel. On the street just outside the Center, a group from one of the teen gangs appeared repeatedly to terrorize all who tried to enter.

For a short while each evening, Myra was alone at the Center, and it seemed that the gang chose to harass her as well, banging on the doors and calling out obscenities.

One night when the gang appeared Myra suddenly felt inspired to tell them about Jesus. Knowing the danger, she first prayed for guidance. Yes, she felt sure she had heard the Lord correctly. She opened the door and walked outside.

The gang moved around her and, keeping her voice steady, she spoke to them about Jesus.

Instead of listening to her, however, the gang shouted threats of drowning her in the nearby river. Trying to appear calm, Myra walked back through the door of the Center and shut it. They did not follow her.

The next evening they were back, once again banging on the door and threatening her life. Still believing she should try and reach out to them,

Myra breathed a prayer to Jesus, asking Him to let the angels of the Lord accompany and protect her as she obeyed Him.

She opened the doorway and was about to speak when the gang members suddenly stopped their shouting, turned to look at one another, and left silently and quickly. Myra had no idea why.

The gang did not return for several days. Then one afternoon, to the surprise of everyone, they entered the Center in an orderly and cooperative fashion.

Much later, after a relationship of trust had been built with the gang, Louis Torres asked them what had made them drop their threats against Myra and leave so peacefully that night.

One young man spoke up. "We wouldn't dare touch her after her boyfriend showed up. That dude had to be seven feet tall."

"I didn't know Myra had a boyfriend," replied Louis thoughtfully. "But at any rate, she was here alone that night."

"No, we saw him," insisted another gang member. "He was right behind her, big as life in his classy white suit."

As Louis Torres finished his story, I recognized the gap principle at work. Myra's actions fit the criteria for angelic intervention that I had drawn from the Old Testament account of Elijah: acting obediently, unselfishly, and with a desire to honor the Lord. Then, even though she appeared to be in danger, an angel stood behind her, keeping her safe.

I noticed, too, that the angels who protect us are

fully capable physically of carrying out their orders. Often those who see angels describe them as enormous beings, "big as life."

If size is any indication of power, we should never worry about their ability to protect us. Imagine this sight: "David looked up and saw the angel of the Lord standing between heaven and earth, with a drawn sword in his hand" (1 Chronicles 21:16). If angels are God's enforcers, then their weapons must be tremendous and versatile. Angels can silence the angry threats of a city gang simply by appearing ... or divert the natural instincts of hungry lions with a word.

The story of Daniel in the lion's den is a wonderful biblical picture of God's protective angels bringing safety in times of danger.

The administrators of King Darius of Babylon were jealous of the favor shown Daniel, their fellow administrator and a Jew, and wanted to be rid of him. They tricked the king into declaring the worship of God a capital offense. Anyone disobeying the command would be thrown into the lion's den, a deep, stone-lined pit full of starved lions, which meant certain death.

Daniel knew full well what consequences he would face by continuing his prayers three times a day, but he chose to obey God regardless. And as soon as he was observed, he was arrested and thrown to the lions.

The next day when Darius hurried to the pit to see what had become of his favorite administrator, he found him alive and well. He was informed by

Daniel: "My God sent his angel, and he shut the mouths of the lions. They have not hurt me."

I don't believe that the angel wrestled with the lions physically and muzzled them. I think the Lord sent them down with the message, "Go have a word with those lions." Then the angel dropped down, touched each one on the nose and said, "Don't you touch Daniel. He's the beloved of the Lord." The angel's authority caused the lions to submit. I personally believe those starved lions would rather go hungry than disobey God's angel.

When the king saw the miraculous results of the angel's intervention, he declared that the entire kingdom would worship the God whom Daniel served. Daniel had stood in the gap between danger and safety out of obedience to God, putting his life in the Lord's hands, and had witnessed His angel at work.

Because of Daniel and the protecting angel, the entire Babylonian kingdom had the opportunity to worship God freely. Many of us forget the influence we have by standing firmly where God wants us and allowing His angels to help us. But some have discovered that help and, as a result, have brought the powerful message of salvation into dangerous situations.

While my husband was president of Southern Asia Bible College in Bangalore, India, a number of years ago, he found that many people there were open to the gospel because of the influence of one Christian man. Records dating from 1929 tell the remarkable story of the angelic assistance Sundar

Singh experienced in Tibet while standing in the gap between danger and safety.

Once when Singh was preaching about Jesus in a public marketplace, he was arrested by a guard from a nearby Buddhist monastery, who was jealous of his influence. The guard brought him on false charges before the Lama, a local magistrate known for his hatred of Christians.

Singh was tried by the Lama, sentenced to death, and dragged mercilessly to the edge of a deep well shaft. The Lama drew aside his heavy robes and pulled out a key permanently attached by a chain to his sash. Ceremoniously, he unlocked the lid and held the key until he could lock the lid shut and return it to his sash.

Strong arms lifted the lid and threw Singh down into the pit. He hit the bottom, stunned by the sickening stench of dead bodies. Then he heard the lid being secured and locked. There was no chance of his climbing out even if the lid had been unlocked. One of his arms was fractured, and besides, the walls of the well were sheer and impossible to climb.

Hours, then days passed. Just when Singh thought he could not endure another moment of his prison, he heard the key turn in the lock high above his head. Had the Lama sentenced another prisoner to death? The rusty hinge groaned, and suddenly stars shone in a dark sky overhead. Singh was startled by something rough brushing against his face. It was a rope. The end was looped, and Singh, though weak, was able to slip his leg into it and grasp it with his good arm. Slowly he was drawn up the shaft and out into the cool night. Collapsing on the ground, grateful to fill his lungs with fresh air, he looked around, but his deliverer had vanished. Painfully Singh crawled home to have his wounds tended and to sleep. In the morning, somewhat fortified, he returned to the marketplace to preach.

Within an hour he was seized once again by angry monks and carried again to the Lama for questioning.

"How did you get free?" demanded the enraged Lama. "Who stole the key to the lock? Explain before something worse happens to you."

Quietly Sundar Singh said, "It was an angel."

"You are lying," shouted the Lama. "Someone must have broken the key off my ring. It is the only one that will turn the lock." With that the Lama pulled aside his heavy robes and drew the chain from his waist. "Tell me who . . ." he was bellowing, when his voice trailed off and a disbelieving look crossed his face.

"Take this man away," he said. "Set him free."

There on the chain was the key.

Amazing? Truly the work of angels is miraculous, even unbelievable, until we remember who they work for. Nothing is impossible for God. He is fully able to keep His children safe in the midst of danger, and equip angels for their assignments. In this case the angel arrived with a rope, the power to unlock a heavy stone lid, and the strength to pull Singh out of the pit.

The angel in a more recent account not only

exhibited his authority, he appeared and spoke to the one he was helping.

Henry Garlock of Springfield, Missouri, was working as a missionary in Africa when he learned that a young female co-worker had been kidnapped by a hostile tribe. Without thought of his own personal safety, Henry went after her, and was captured almost immediately by the same tribe. When he found that the tribe would release the woman for a certain amount of money, Henry agreed to pay it.

On the way back to the missionary compound, however, the tribe again overtook Henry, and this time threatened to kill him. They passed the tribal death sentence on him and took him to their place of execution in the jungle. But Henry spoke to them with assurance.

"If my God is alive," he said, "He will send an angel to deliver me." The tribesmen laughed at him, and in response forced his head down on the trunk of a tree, underneath the executioner's axe.

Henry sensed that the executioner had lifted the axe, then heard him gasp. After a shuffle he heard the native shout, "It's an angel!" The axe fell harmlessly to the ground. Henry lifted his head and saw the tribesmen running away. Now, where the executioner had stood was an angel of the Lord, shining and powerful.

"You are free to go home," the angel said. "I have stopped the execution."

Gratefully, Henry rose and walked back to the compound.

Henry Garlock's story shows me clearly that if we walk in the will of God, we can claim angelic protection when we are in danger, although the moment we step out of God's will, I believe we part company with angels.

Perhaps I should stress that people being helped by angels are acting in obedience to God, not setting out to follow their own wills, or—worse—to test the Lord by charging into a dangerous situation and watching to see how He will pull them out. Good intentions are not a substitute for obedience. It is too easy to rush ahead of God and bring on all sorts of difficulties. We must wait for His leading, then act obediently.

One couple who did exactly this—and who were delivered by angelic material provision—were Mr. and Mrs. Kenneth Ware, Americans living in Paris during World War II.

The Wares were horrified to hear that Jews were being taken from their homes, loaded like cattle onto trains, and transported to camps where they faced death in the gas ovens. The Wares could not have known that six million Jews would eventually lose their lives in these camps, but they believed God was leading them to help as many as they could. So they began the perilous task of secretly hiding Jews, feeding them, praying with them, and helping them escape under the cover of darkness to countries where they would be safe.

Food was rationed so strictly that at one point the Wares had no supplies left in the house and no means of replenishing their empty cupboards. They had spent what money they had, and buying on credit was impossible. Besides, they did not want to draw attention to themselves with the quantity of food they needed.

Believing God could still meet their needs, they decided to write out a shopping list in the form of a prayer. Mrs. Ware got out paper and pencil and made a list of everything she needed: meat, apples, carrots, her preferred brand of flour, and many other supplies. Then the Wares knelt together to pray.

A knock at the door brought them both to their feet.

"Who is it?" called out Mr. Ware.

"Please let me in," responded a soft, urgent voice.

Thinking someone must be in need, Mr. Ware opened the door and was surprised to see a tall man dressed in white.

"I have the items your wife ordered," he said, setting two bags down on the table.

"But there must be some mistake," responded Mr. Ware, shutting the door. He looked in wonder at his wife who was removing from the bags every item she had written on her prayer list. Everything was there, down to the brand of flour she had specified.

When they both looked up to thank the man, they realized, to their astonishment—though only seconds had passed and the door remained closed—he was gone. The stranger had left even more mysteriously than he had appeared.

Rejoicing, the Wares knew that an angel of the Lord had brought their provisions. No one else had known their needs, or would even have had that kind of supply on hand. It also taught them—and me—that angels can provide the most practical kinds of assistance for those to whom they have been sent by God, in response to godly prayer.

In every account we have examined in this chapter, the persons ministered to exhibited courage in the face of obvious danger. An angry tribe is not the safest of neighbors, after all, and a person who harbors anyone else sentenced to death is likely to receive that sentence himself.

But suppose we don't know we are in danger? We might be in what appears to be the safest of circumstances, with no reason to ask for God's help, when in fact we are helpless before an unknown danger. How will angels help us then?

4

RESCUING ANGELS

Jack and Jenny Pate looked up from their renovation work on the second floor of their Texas farmhouse just in time to see their three-year-old daughter lean too hard on the window screen. Jenny opened her mouth to call out when the screen buckled, and with a scream the helpless child slid out into thin air.

Paralyzed for a moment with horror and helplessness, both of them breathed the word, "Jesus!" It was a prayer, a gasp that cut through the terrifying realization that Peggy would land on the concrete steps beneath the window. Nearly stumbling over one another, the Pates rushed down the stairs and out the front door.

Their anguish turned to astonishment when they found Peggy sitting quietly on the bottom step. Scooping her up in her arms, Jenny wept with relief.

"Don't worry, Mommy," piped Peggy, "that big man caught me." Jack and Jenny looked around but saw no one. What man? Where had he come from? Where had he gone? There was no place out there in the open Texas countryside for anyone to hide.

It would have sounded made up except for the fact that Peggy was all right. And when they examined their daughter, they could not find one scratch or bruise. And Peggy did not seem a bit frightened from the experience.

After discussing the incredible event with other members of the family and my husband who was their pastor, Jack and Jenny were directed to Isaiah 63:9: "In all their distress he too was distressed, and the *angel* of his presence *saved* them. In his love and mercy he redeemed them; he *lifted them up* and *carried* them." God must still use angels today, they decided, just as He did in Old Testament times, to rescue His people.

Whether the angel was Peggy's personal guardian angel or one under commission from the throne room, they did not know. But they grasped as never before the meaning of several other verses as well: "Behold, I send an angel before thee, to keep thee in the way" (Exodus 23:20, KJV); and, "In heaven (children's) angels do always behold the face of my Father" (Matthew 18:10, KJV).

Jack and Jenny had been helpless to save their daughter. Their only hope, expressed in the one-word prayer they breathed, had been that Jesus would intervene and protect their child from critical injury, possibly death. Only He could act for them, and they instinctively entrusted their daughter to His care.

What power there is in the name of Jesus! Because Jack and Jenny had often prayed that Jesus would protect Peggy, in that time of emergency they called on His name faster than they could reason what to do. And in answer to that prayer, Jesus sent an angel.

Here is an example of a second gap situation— rescue from helplessness. If we need help and cannot help ourselves, God may send a protective angel to act on our behalf.

Jill Josten, a friend of mine, was in the hospital following the delivery of her first baby. After twenty-three hours of difficult labor, Jill was drained physically. When she stood for the first time to walk from her room to the bathroom, she felt dizzy but certain she could walk by herself. And she made the trip without assistance.

When she came out of the bathroom, however, she sensed suddenly that she had overexerted herself and was going to faint. Casting about for something to hold on to as her knees began to buckle, she saw a male nurse in the hall holding a tray of blood samples, and called out to him. No sooner had she spoken than she saw a flash of white uniform beside her and felt two strong hands under her armpits, supporting her. Then all went black.

When Jill came to she was lying on her hospital bed and the male nurse was standing over her, still holding the tray.

"I'm so glad you heard me," she said weakly. "Thank you for catching me."

The young man shook his head. "I'm sorry. I couldn't get there; I couldn't risk dropping all these blood samples. And I don't think I could have made it in time anyway. I'm just glad you got yourself back to bed. You could have had a hard fall on that tile floor."

When Jill told me the story later, she said, "Betty, if that man didn't help me, it had to be an angel. I saw the flash of white uniform and felt the hands supporting me." She added with a smile, "I guess I know now the meaning of that verse in Psalm 91 about angels lifting you up in their hands!"

Jill, like Peggy's parents, knew she was in need of immediate physical help (though her need was not so acute as theirs), and she was unable to do anything about it. Her prayers for health and safety during her hospital stay had been answered during a gap of helplessness.

I read a similar account in the Terre Haute (Indiana) *Tribune*, except this one involved a life-and-death situation. Two young women were trapped beneath an overturned car on Highway 40 that they feared was about to be engulfed in flames. They prayed frantically.

Then a young man, driving west on Highway 40, saw the women and sensed their danger. He quickly stopped his car and ran over to them, not knowing how he could help them escape. Apparently the car would have to be lifted up so the women could crawl out, and he was without help himself. So as he ran he prayed, "Jesus, give me strength. Help me to help."

He reached the car and with one last prayer put his hands under the bumper and lifted. Miraculously, he held the car up just long enough for the two women to be able to crawl free.

Was it simply an emergency flow of adrenalin that enabled him to lift the heavy car? That may have been the medical analysis the paper reported, but I believe unseen angels worked alongside the man, answering his prayer by helping him do what he was physically unable to accomplish. The Bible says that angels "are stronger and more powerful [than men]" (2 Peter 2:11).

There is one factor these three stories have in common: the sudden awareness of an emergency situation and the need for immediate help. There may be times we do not know an emergency exists until it is too late, as happened with Jack and Jenny Pate; or we may not have enough time to ask the Lord for help, as was the case with my friend Jill. Yet, there may be times we do not even know that some protective measure needs to be taken. What then?

Jim Arnett has learned an answer to that question. Jim and his wife are new friends of mine from Kokomo, Indiana, not far from where I was born.

He told me about a trip he and his father took to Florida. Jim, who was not a Christian at the time, was respectful of his father's faith, but did feel his reliance on God at times was a bit fanatical.

Jim and his father were driving along Interstate 75 on the Florida-Georgia state line when his father said, seemingly out of the blue, "Jim, buckle your seatbelt."

Unaccustomed to using his seatbelt, and curious at his father's tone, he asked why, but his father responded simply, "Never mind. Just *do* it." Jim buckled up and drove on.

Minutes later, Jim told me, he looked into his rear view mirror to see a semi tractor-trailer bearing down on him fast from behind. As the driver started to pull into the left lane to pass Jim's car, it became apparent he had misjudged the speed of his approach, for he did not move to the left in time. His semi struck the rear of Jim's car, knocking it like a toy across the highway and over a twenty-foot embankment.

Apparently a second tractor-trailer, trailing the first, braked and swerved to miss the accident and also ran off the road. For within seconds, Jim said, that second truck hurtled over the embankment, leapfrogged his own car, actually taking the roof off before it crashed to a stop two hundred feet away.

Jim and his father were dazed but all right, incredibly, secure within their seatbelts; and Jim told me later that he realized God had spoken to his father, saving Jim's life.

As if that experience were not enough, a second near-fatal accident only three months later introduced him to the idea that an angel must be protecting him.

He was driving a van, safely buckled into his

seatbelt, on a highway not far from his home. Directly in front of him a heavy truck was transporting steel. Behind him, visible in his rear view mirror, he watched as a flatbed truck gained on him, fully loaded with large logs. Jim told me he began to feel claustrophobic—probably in good part a result of his frightening accident on the Florida trip.

"I tried to dismiss my fears," he said, "but I was sandwiched between these two trucks and I felt uncomfortable. I would have passed the steel truck, except I was in a no-passing zone."

Suddenly Jim felt a large, heavy hand over his on the steering wheel, and he heard an inner voice order, *Pull quickly into the left lane.* For a fraction of a second he thought about the yellow line on his side that told him he was in a no-passing zone; yet at the command of the hand over his he swerved the van left.

Jim was not quite all the way into the passing lane when he heard the crash. The flatbed behind him had apparently had brake failure, and he watched, horrified, as it smashed into the truck ahead. If Jim had not been helped by that strong hand on the wheel, his light van would have been squeezed like an accordion between those two heavy trucks.

Since that experience, Jim tells me that he and his wife have both met Jesus as their Lord. They are grateful that angels ministered to Jim through the prayers of his father and others, when he had no knowledge or control of imminent, life-threatening danger.

The gap of helplessness for the Christian seems closely tied in with faith. We cannot know every perilous instance ahead of time to pray about, but we can trust to the watchcare of our heavenly Father. He does not guarantee across-the-board freedom from mishaps between here and eternity, but He does promise to lead us where He wants us, and care for us along the way.

We, in turn, must learn to hear His voice and stay within His will. Jim, unlike little Peggy's parents and my friend Jill, committed his life to Jesus Christ only when he saw firsthand the miracle-working power of God. But it is not up to us to predict the circumstances in which the Lord will intervene in the life of an unbeliever; only to trust in His ability to care for *us*.

An experience that happened to one of my brothers taught me about this kind of trust. Before any trip Marvin takes, even before turning the motor on, he prays, just as our dad prayed when we were small, that God will protect the passengers and send angels for safety on the way.

Several years ago Marvin, his wife, Sharon, and their two children were driving north of Jacksonville, Florida, when the indicator in his car showed the engine overheating. Getting out and raising the hood, he knew better than to take off the radiator cap, as steam was hissing around it. He decided to prop the hood open until the engine cooled.

But as he was lifting it up, the radiator cap suddenly blew off. The force of the pent-up steam and the scalding fluid knocked him to the ground and burned him from his waist to the top of his head.

Sharon ran to a nearby house and called an ambulance. Marvin was rushed to the nearest emergency room where a burn specialist was waiting for him. Upon examining him, the doctor exclaimed how fortunate it was that Marvin had been wearing glasses, and Marvin assured him he didn't wear glasses.

"You must have been wearing sunglasses, then," he persisted.

"But I wasn't."

The doctor shook his head. "All I know," he said at last, "is that an angel must have put his hands over your eyes. Your ears, nose, even the inside of your mouth, are all burned, but your eyes have had some kind of protective covering."

As I listened to my brother's story by telephone, recounted from his hospital bed, my heart was thankful for the preservation of Marvin's vision. But even more, I was awestruck at the Lord's faithfulness to guard His children in times of helplessness. Our entire family believed the doctor had spoken the truth about an angel shielding Marvin's eyes. This could only have been God's answer to his prayer for angelic protection. And the proof of this protection—Marvin's eyesight—left me with a better understanding of heavenly intervention in another kind of gap situation.

The Lord has directed us to pray for our needs, since protection in a hazardous world is a legitimate concern. But we must be careful to avoid the paranoia that says we have to cover every possible circumstance with prayer. Marvin prayed for safety for their trip, but he didn't mention every moving piece of the engine by name, or every intersection, or every traffic light. Our prayers should be thorough but not ridiculous.

The Lord has told us to pray, but He has also told us to trust. If we let Him lead our prayers, we will not fall into the danger of considering angels "good luck charms" whose power we have to invoke minute by minute, or face the consequences.

The Bible tells us there are millions of angels at God's command in times of crisis. What a comforting thought! And if God's children face potential trouble more than we realize, God's angels have probably protected us more often than we realize from what might have been. Sometimes we can help ourselves. Sometimes God uses another person to answer our prayers. But on the occasions when we are helpless unless He helps us, He may send angels to deliver, fight for, or minister to us.

I should not have been surprised several years back to turn on a television program and hear a prominent movie star tell how helplessness had been swept from his life and the weight of suicidal thoughts lifted because of a mysterious angelic visitor.

The actor was Mickey Rooney, and he told about the extent to which he had hit bottom. Already fighting depression, he had just starred in *Bill*, perhaps the greatest film of his career, which left him more depressed than before. Where could he go from there? Then his eighth wife left him. He felt there was no fulfillment for him anywhere; that he was a failure. As time went on, he began to lose the desire to live.

Walking into a restaurant, almost hopeless about alleviating his terrifying loneliness, he slumped into a booth and ordered a bowl of soup. He lay his head in his arms, too depressed and lonely to care about anything.

In a few moments he felt the gentle pressure of a hand on his shoulder. Supposing that the waitress had brought his soup, he lifted his head and started to lean back against the seat. When he realized the hand still rested on his shoulder, as if to get his attention, he looked up and met the gaze of a young waiter dressed in a white uniform.

"Sir, I have a message for you." The young man spoke with conviction and sincerity. "The Lord Jesus Christ asked me to tell you that He loves you very much and that you will experience great joy from Him."

Then he turned and walked away.

At once Mickey felt inexplicable contentment and peace. Waves of joy gushed through him. For the first time in a long time, he felt hope. After a moment he slipped from the booth to find the young waiter and thank him. But he found only the head waiter, who told him—to his astonishment—that no one employed by the restaurant fit the description of that young man.

Mickey walked back to his booth, filled with happiness. As he stated on the television program,

"I know I had the message delivered to me directly from Jesus by an angel."

He went on, because of that encounter, to receive Jesus as his personal Savior, and to marry a woman who shares his Christian commitment. "For the first time in my life," he says, " I know what real love is, because God is love, and we have Him in the center of our marriage and our lives."

Had God cared enough for Mickey Rooney to assign an individual angel to protect him from possible suicide? Through the godly errand of this messenger, whoever he was, Mickey's life was set in a new, hope-filled direction: from confusion and despair to a decision to follow Christ. The greatest rescue of all is the saving of a lost and helpless soul.

Had someone been praying for Mickey Rooney? Undoubtedly. What a reminder for us as Christians! How many people have been left without hope when our prayers could have made a difference? We would do well not only to pray for our own protection, but for those who need to be rescued—perhaps even by an angel—in a moment of helplessness.

5

ANGELS AND INTERCESSION

I have been aware all my life of the inestimable power of prayer, but after hearing hundreds of accounts of how God met people at their point of need, I have come to see something of the role angels play in answering these prayers. I have come to believe, for example, that when we pray, angels battle for us in an important gap, bringing answers to our prayers of intercession for believers and nonbelievers alike.

In so doing, they may act not only against whatever prevents an unsaved individual from salvation, but against whatever opposes a believer in fulfilling God's directives for his life.

It is vitally important to intercede, knowing that Jesus responds to need. The apostle Paul assured the church at Colosse that "since the day we heard about you, we have not stopped praying for you"

(Colossians 1:9); and he had such concern for his unsaved Jewish brothers that he had "great sorrow and unceasing anguish in my heart" (Romans 9:2).

If we, too, are gravitating toward the needs of others, God will endorse our work. I have been particularly impressed with two accounts of angels working in the lives of non-Christians through the intercession of Christians.

The first account involves T.J. and Maureen O'Bannon, who were living in quaint Gatlinburg, Tennessee, during the Great Depression. It was Christmastime, but the peacefulness of the snowy Christmas card scene outside their home contrasted with the inner unrest they were both experiencing.

T.J., for his part, was rebelling against oppressive economic privations by joining his brother in plundering and stealing; while Maureen, devastated by the change in her husband, pleaded with him to change his lifestyle. She would rather have him safe at home with her, she told him, than have all the money in the world. But T.J. insisted he would be a good provider for her, no matter what it took.

When he and his brother learned that the railroad office would be holding the payroll and cash receipts over the holiday, they determined to break in. As they formed their plans, Maureen prayed faithfully for her husband: "Whatever it takes, Lord, bring him to You."

The nighttime break-in went as planned. But just as his brother was securing the money in the rumble seat of their Model T Ford, T.J. heard the sound of a police siren cut through the darkness. He ran for the automobile, but saw he couldn't make it. He shouted for his brother to drive off, then fell to the ground as a bullet grazed his left cheek.

When he refused to reveal the identity of his accomplice or the whereabouts of the money, T.J. was convicted of the robbery alone and sent to prison. The money, he and his brother agreed, would remain hidden. Maureen visited him as often as she could, and prayed for him constantly.

Three Christmases later, the hard shell around T.J.'s heart began to crack. He awoke at three one morning with an overwhelming desire to make his peace with God. If only he could get to the prison chapel and pray!

"O God," he called aloud through his tears, "have mercy on me." Then he called for a guard, hoping he could convince him to take him to the chapel, despite the lateness of the hour.

A silent, bearded guard appeared, one other than the regular night guard, whom T.J. did not recognize. He seemed old for such a job—indeed, his silvery hair appeared almost radiant—but the twinkle in his silver-blue eyes distinguished him as alert and capable.

Wordlessly the guard opened the cell door and walked beside T.J. to the chapel. Once there, T.J. fell across the altar and asked Jesus to forgive him. The guard, kneeling silently alongside, put his arm around T.J.'s shoulders until T.J. was ready to return to the confinement of his cell. He was peaceful at last in the new freedom of God's forgiveness.

But before the elderly guard could reopen the cell door, they heard shouts. Two uniformed guards ran down the passage, grabbed T.J., and threw him into his cell.

"How did you get out?" they demanded through the bars. "Were you trying to escape?"

"Of course not," responded T.J. "This guard accompanied me to the chapel." But when he looked to his bearded friend for confirmation, the elderly guard had disappeared.

T.J. described him to the others as best he could remember, but neither believed him. One stated flatly that in twenty-six years in that institution he had never worked with an older, bearded guard with silver hair.

Later in the spring, when his trial was reviewed before a judge, T.J. agreed to return the money to the railroad. He was released under parole and allowed to go home. He and Maureen are now retired and living in Tuscon, Arizona. T.J. speaks at prison chapels, extends financial help to young people who want to attend Bible school, and continues to share his personal experience with an angel to help others find Jesus' forgiveness.

And all because Maureen had demonstrated one of the keys to successful intercession for salvation: She persevered. God does not force anyone to make a decision against his will, but neither does He stop dealing with a person as long as someone is persevering in prayer about him. Eventually, I believe, the person being prayed for will relinquish sinful desires in order to find the peace God has for him.

Did an angel help T. J. O'Bannon in his moment of desperation? I have no doubt: surely a ministering angel was sent to meet the need of this lost soul in response to his wife's intercession, just as the writer to the Hebrews described: "[God] makes his angels winds, his servants flames of fire" (Hebrews 1:7). Maureen had never given up hope that the Lord would act, and continued to pray for T.J.'s salvation no matter how grim the circumstances. Because of Maureen's perseverance, an angel was able to help T.J. break through the hardness of heart that would keep him from salvation.

As we endure in our own prayers, we can take courage in the fact that the angels of the Lord take up swords and fight along with us.

T.J.'s is not the first reported instance, of course, of an angel appearing to a prison inmate. The apostles in the early church were actually freed from jail through the ministrations of an angel. Luke recounts: "An angel of the Lord opened the doors of the jail and brought them out"(Acts 5:19).

A second, modern-day account that has impressed me involves the Reverend Steve Wood, pastor of the Dakota Alliance Church in Sisseton, South Dakota. Steve's parents began praying when he was young that he would know Jesus as His personal Savior and find God's direction for his life. They believed, he tells me now, that God has a "divine design" for every person.

One day during his boyhood years, he and a friend were taking a long walk, talking about the future, when they were joined by a dignified elderly gentleman. They liked him instantly, and allowed the conversation to turn to spiritual matters. He encouraged them to give their lives to Jesus early and trust Him for their future plans.

Steve and his friend were fascinated with their companion's voice and his mannerisms. Something else impressed them, too—the fact that although they were walking up a steep hill, and the boys were panting for breath, the man walked effortlessly, not appearing tired at all.

The instant Steve and his friend realized there was something supernatural about their companion, he vanished before their eyes.

The impact of their angelic visitor left quite an impression on the boys. Each dedicated his life to Christ as a result, and vowed to follow His will.

Now, as an Alliance pastor, Steve often emphasizes how important it is for parents to intercede, or stand in the gap, for their children, even though it may be someone else who brings those children to the point of decision to follow after God. That someone may even be an angel—not at all an outrageous idea if we allow the New Testament to remind us of those people who "have entertained angels without knowing it" (Hebrews 13:2).

This brings us to the second way angels may help us in the gap of intercession. Not only will they work to bring unbelievers to the point of salvation, but they will fight against whatever would keep believers from fulfilling God's directives for their lives, be it a physical or spiritual barrier.

My friend Gloria Lundstrom, whose brother-in-law leads a traveling evangelistic ministry, told me about the time angels provided her and her family with physical protection in answer to intercessory prayer.

One snowy December evening in 1984 she and her family, along with the Lowell Lundstrom evangelistic team, were en route from one town in Montana to another, believing that God was directing them to go there. They were traveling in a bus and pulling a heavy trailer loaded with sound equipment.

Snow continued to fall as Gloria's husband, Larry, drove late that night through the mountains. Just as they reached the top of a mountain pass and were proceeding slowly down the other side, they ran into freezing rain. The icy pavement made it impossible for the bus to maintain traction, and before they knew what was happening, it began to slide out of control toward the road's edge. There were no guardrails, and since they were at the very top of the pass, the narrow road dropped off into a sheer expanse on *both* sides, plunging downward for thousands of feet.

Larry struggled with the wheel, and Gloria began to whisper over and over, "O Jesus, O Jesus. We plead the blood of Jesus over this bus and over all our lives. Lord, send Your guardian angels to protect us. In the name of Jesus we pray."

While she prayed, she looked out the window and felt there was no way out; the bus was sliding toward the edge. Just when she was certain they would plunge over the side, she felt a kind of impact, as though the bus were a rolling ball that had been pushed gently back to the middle of the road. Then, when it slid to the other side of the road, Gloria felt the same sensation and was astonished to see that the bus had again somehow stayed on the road.

This went on, back and forth, until they had traveled a seemingly endless half-a-mile and Larry was finally able to stop the coach on the steep grade.

"Thank you, Jesus!" Gloria exclaimed. "Larry, park this rig until spring!"

She told me later she felt totally unnerved, and as the family and team gathered together in the front of the bus, they knew God had intervened to spare their lives.

What they did not know was that someone had been interceding on their behalf. The next night Gloria called her mother, who asked immediately, "How were the roads and weather last night?"

"Terrible," Gloria responded, and then listened spellbound as her mother continued.

"Well, the Lord woke me up last night with an urgency to pray. I began to pray and right away, just like in a dream, I saw your bus with a deep ravine on either side. I began to pray for God's protection for all of you and I saw the most amazing thing: A band of angels surrounded the bus! And do you know what? It was as if the angels were "playing" a serious game. When the bus would veer to the right edge one group would "bunt" it back onto the road. Then it would slide to the left edge and the other angels would "bunt" it back."

"But Mom, that's exactly what we felt in the bus!"

Then they rejoiced together over the Lord's goodness, Gloria told me later, and she reminded me of Psalm 34:7: "The angel of the Lord encampeth round about them that fear him, and delivereth them" (KJV). That is exactly what happened when an intercessor prayed. The prayers of Gloria's mother had been answered immediately: Angels were commissioned in that exact moment of need.

One spring not too long ago I spoke to a large, thriving congregation at Bible Center Church in Evansville, Indiana. The church not only ministered to the attending congregation, but televised the services for area viewers, and has even established churches in foreign countries. I became interested in the growth of the ministry, and found a fascinating account in the book *I Met an Angel*, written by the pastor, the Reverend A. D. Van Hoose, with Rod Spence.

When the church first began to grow, the pastor feared he would not be able to cope with the extent of the work God was doing. He doubted his abilities to handle it all. The congregation was growing; there were miracles evidenced in services; and a new construction program became necessary to accommodate the congregation's growing needs.

One day Pastor Van Hoose went into his office and locked the door. He needed to hear from God that he was indeed the man for that job. He fell on his face, and for forty grueling minutes asked God to either assure him or free him from a responsibility he felt incapable of handling.

Finally, exhausted, he felt a release. As he sat down in his desk chair, he felt another presence in the room. Mustering up courage he declared, "Reveal yourself!"

A chair placed near the end of his desk suddenly became white with light except for a tiny black dot in the center. The dot began to grow, and he heard the sound of an object moving from a great distance toward him with tremendous speed. It seemed to explode outward, and in the blink of an eye the dot had become a man—the most handsome, dynamic-looking man he had ever seen.

Pastor Van Hoose did not notice how his visitor was dressed because he couldn't take his eyes off his face with its strong, sharply chiseled features and an aura of nobility.

The angel spoke at once. "Your prayers have been heard and you are going to be used. I am sent of God to instruct you. Listen carefully to what I have to say."

The angel then talked with Pastor Van Hoose about his life and his work, explaining various developments that would occur, and making clear that he was not being released from the ministry. Instead, he would continue to be used to lift up the name of Jesus, and to help the sick and needy.

Then the light that was the angel began swirling in a reverse direction from the one in which he had come. He shrank back into a small dot that finally disappeared, whirling back with the accompanying light, leaving the pastor blinking and open-mouthed from the staggering encounter.

It was not long before the prophecies of the angel came true. Attendance at the church grew, its television stations opened, and mission opportunities came along with the finances to develop them—all without going into debt.

The message from the angel, applicable to all of us, was this: Do not fear to do what God has commissioned you to do. All of us are called to pray for the needs of others, and we should persevere until we learn the answer.

Sometimes it seems that angels are not dispatched as quickly as we would like. As in the case of interceding for someone for salvation, however, we must persevere.

A second experience involving the prophet Daniel and an angel should offer a good reminder to all of us standing in a gap of intercession for someone else. Daniel knew how to prevail in prayer, as we can see: "I, Daniel, mourned for three weeks. I ate no choice food; no meat or wine touched my lips" (Daniel 10:2).

Notice what the angel, when he finally arrived, said to Daniel: "Do not be afraid, Daniel. Since the first day that you set your mind to gain understanding and to humble yourself before your God, your words were heard, and I have come in response to them. But the prince of the Persian kingdom resisted me twenty-one days. Then Michael, one of the chief princes, came to help me, because I was detained there with the king of Persia" (verses 12–13).

The angel had left heaven with the answer on the first day Daniel prayed, and fought for three weeks to break through the barriers of the opposing forces of Satan. When he was joined in the battle by the great archangel Michael, he was freed and able to deliver the message.

Suppose Daniel had given up and stopped praying for his nation before the angel was able to fight his way through the opponents. Would the retracted prayer have meant that the angel was left without the powerful support of intercession? Would the angel have had a more difficult struggle against the powers that tried to hold him back? If Daniel had lost faith in the Lord's ability to answer, I doubt he would have heard the answer, even if the angel could have made it through the enemy's stronghold. We may never know of the prayers that might have been answered had we not given up so soon.

I wonder what God would do for our nation if all Christians would worship God—truly worship Him as Daniel did three times a day. Angels are responsible for the protection of nations, to see that neither the devil nor evil men spoil God's program; but our intercessory backing is vitally important to their role. We should learn to follow Daniel's example.

He not only hung on until the powers that resisted him were defeated, but he supplemented his determined prayer with fasting. I have found that when we deny our bodies food, the discomfort in our stomachs serves as a constant reminder of our need to pray diligently. There is no virtue in starving without faith. We could make the decision to lie down and refuse food until we died, and it would accomplish nothing. But when we combine self-denial with faith and prayer, it produces power that will propel our prayers more forcefully than before—sometimes with astonishing results.

The apostle Paul wrote, "For our struggle is not against flesh and blood, but against the rulers, against the authorities, against the powers of this dark world and against the spiritual forces of evil in the heavenly realms" (Ephesians 6:12). Satan's forces would like to defeat us, hinder our prayers, and hurt our loved ones, but *we are not powerless*. The weapons of our warfare "have divine power to demolish strongholds" (2 Corinthians 10:4). The psalmist David wrote of his own enemies, "May they be like chaff before the wind, with the angel of the Lord pursuing them" (Psalm 35:5).

We do well to ask God to give us the desire to pray until the victory is won. A stranger seeking his fortune in the California Gold Rush was said to have been found dead with this note attached to his pick: "I give up." Later, discovered just eleven feet from his body, was the richest gold strike in the history of the West. So ask God for courage and determination not to give up or give in to the forces that come against you. For we know that the angels of the Lord will go to battle to fight for our good causes when we pray, as they did for Daniel. It might even help to think of prayer as our Christian obligation.

Don't give up short of the answer. Stand in the gap of intercession, and you will find the angels of the Lord taking up swords and fighting for you.

6

MESSENGER
ANGELS

One of the first things I learned about angels is that the word itself means *courier, messenger, ambassador*. I would assume, therefore, that most of their missions involve relaying messages from God for our instruction. Does this mean that at the times we are indecisive about what God wants us to do, angels might arrive with the answer?

Such seemed to be the case with Mark Buntain who, with his wife, Huldah, have worked for twenty-six years, and are still working, to establish a church, a hospital, and an orphanage in Calcutta, India.

One summer season the monsoon rains were particularly destructive, and Mark grew afraid as flooding threatened to destroy what they had worked so long to build. The government declared Calcutta a disaster area and began evacuations.

After seeing his wife and those under his care taken to safety, Mark himself boarded a small commercial plane and slid into an aisle seat next to an empty window seat. He was glad to be sitting alone because of the grief weighing on him so heavily.

As the plane taxied and took off, Mark wondered if the years of sacrifice had been in vain. Would everything he and his wife had worked for be washed away? And what about those who had not been able to be airlifted out of the flood areas? He prayed silently for them.

His thoughts were interrupted when a well-dressed man stepped from the aisle and sat down beside him. As the stranger began to talk, he revealed uncanny insight into Mark's fears about his work in India, although Mark had neither introduced himself nor mentioned his worries. The stranger discussed the future of India and encouraged Mark not to be afraid. He even offered him practical steps for the future.

Courage welled up in Mark's heart as he began to believe that all would indeed be well, that God was protecting his ministry, and that he would continue his mission work in Calcutta.

While they were talking, a stewardess stopped by Mark's seat to take orders for refreshments. He ordered a soft drink, then turned to see if his new seatmate wanted anything. There was no one beside him.

Agitated, Mark got up and tried to find him. He looked in the restroom and into every face along either side of the aisle of the small plane. The well-dressed man was nowhere to be found. When Mark asked the stewardess if she had seen him sitting there, she said she had not; and after checking the number of passengers, she confirmed that the correct number was currently on board. The well-dressed man was not among them.

They were miles above earth. Where had the stranger come from, and where had he gone? Mark knew only that he had been visited by an angel with a special message and that he should go back to his work with confidence.

Several days later, when he returned to Calcutta, he found everything just as the gentleman had predicted and was grateful for the angel's instructions as he struggled in the gap of indecision.

Probably the most important message ever delivered was the one brought by the angel Gabriel to the virgin Mary, which placed Joseph in a terrible place of indecision in need of an answer from God.

Gabriel had been sent by God to announce to Mary that she was to give birth to Jesus, the Messiah. He greeted her with these words: "Greetings, you who are highly favored! The Lord is with you" (Luke 1:28).

The Gospel writer Luke tells us that Mary was troubled at this. Truly, it would be a shock for any young girl suddenly to have a majestic herald appear and announce God's favor! Yet verse 29 of Luke 1 says Mary was "greatly troubled" not at his presence but at his *words*. Perhaps true humility or

a heart free from pride had kept her from considering herself as one especially worthy of favor.

In any case, Gabriel put her fears at rest. "Do not
be afraid, Mary: you have found favor with God,"
he told her. "You will be with child and give birth
to a son, and you are to give him the name Jesus.
He will be great and will be called the Son of the
Most High . . ." (Luke 1:30-32).

Again we see Mary's humble nature in her
response. She did not ask why she had been chosen,
nor what it was about her that pleased the Lord.
Rather, she asked how this amazing thing was to
come about since, as she explained, she was a
virgin. The angel responded that the power of the
Most High would "overshadow" her and that she
would conceive.

Notice the difference between Mary's response
and that of Zechariah when the angel Gabriel told
him his wife would bear a child who would "make
ready a people prepared for the Lord" (Luke 1:17).
Mary's response—"How will this be?"—shows
curious and expectant faith. She did not doubt its
possibility; she simply wondered how the Lord
would bring it about.

Zechariah, on the other hand, expressed doubt
and the need for proof: "How can I be sure of this?
I am an old man and my wife is well along in
years." He did not get the kind of proof he probably
expected. The angel declared, "I am Gabriel. I
stand in the presence of God, and I have been sent
to speak to you and to tell you this good news. And
now you will be silent and not able to speak until

the day this happens, because you did not believe my words, which will come true at their proper time" (Luke 1:19-20).

When one of the Lord's hosts comes to us with a clear directive, we are well advised to believe him.

Mary accepted the word of the angel. After he left she did not boast to her friends that she had been divinely chosen, but pondered these and many other things in her heart. I am amazed at Mary's obedience, her submission to God's will, and her willingness to listen to the angel's message.

When it became evident to the townspeople that Mary was pregnant, her betrothed, Joseph, entered a terrible state of indecision. Apparently much time had already elapsed. He loved Mary, but probably found her explanation hard to believe. Should he marry her or not? What would people think? Would they accuse him of being immoral? He was in a turmoil of indecision, and in need of counsel. Finally, hoping to save her any more public humiliation, he decided to divorce Mary quietly— not the choice the Lord wanted him to make. Joseph needed redirection if he were to follow God's will.

Matthew tells us, "But after he had considered this, an angel of the Lord appeared to him in a dream and said, 'Joseph son of David, do not be afraid to take Mary home as your wife, because what is conceived in her is from the Holy Spirit'" (Matthew 1:20). After that message, Joseph never again questioned Mary's faithfulness. (The first marriage counselor was an angel!)

The angels continued to give Mary and Joseph instruction. After the birth of Jesus in Bethlehem, where Joseph had been obligated to register for the census, they learned from the Magi that the jealous king Herod was inquiring about the Child. Again Joseph needed direction, and again an angel of the Lord spoke to him in a dream, telling him to take the mother and child, flee into Egypt, and remain there until he received word that it was safe.

When wicked Herod realized that he had been outwitted, he was furious. He gave orders for all the boys in and near Bethlehem who were two years old and under to be killed, hoping that one of them would be the Christ Child. But Jesus was safe through His parents' willingness to obey God through His messenger angels.

This account of Mary and Joseph shows us as perhaps no other passage of Scripture the important role of angels as messengers, and how vital it is that we believe their messages. Because Mary and Joseph accepted what the angel said as being directly from God, they acted on it and thus preserved God's plan of salvation for the world. Had they not listened, the baby Jesus might have been one of the infants slain—in which case, would we have been lost for eternity without any way to be reconciled to God?

If angels so control the affairs of men, both now and in the future, the messages they bring us must be important, not only from our perspective of needing to know what to do, but from the larger perspective of God's will at work in the world. I am continually impressed with God's goodness and grateful for His desire to "work all things together for good" (Romans 8:28).

Elden Lawrence, a handsome Sioux Indian who lived near us in South Dakota, told me about his personal experience of receiving guidance from an angel and the good it worked in his life.

From the time he was a child, the poverty and helplessness of his people on the Indian reservation had thrown a shroud of despair over him. For escape, his family brewed a whiskey concoction in their home and spent every weekend trying to lose their misery in drunkenness. They even mixed the alcohol with orange Kool-Aid for the children.

It was little wonder Elden became an alcoholic. When as a young adult he left the reservation, he drank away his days, spent his nights in railroad cars, and ate in charity houses and soup kitchens.

One evening he was robbed and beaten by four men in a bar who left him for dead. He does not know how long he was unconscious before he was discovered and carried to a rescue mission, where an amazing thing happened. Somehow the love and caring of the people there touched a spot of longing within him, and one night he had a special dream.

He saw two frightened children, a boy and girl he did not know, crossing a railroad bridge alone. He sensed they were in danger and watched as an angel appeared to help them. Elden, understanding the angel's example, walked up to the two children, took each of them by the hand, and walked them to safety.

When he awoke he found he had undergone an internal transformation: He wanted to be free once and for all from the bondage of alcohol, and he longed for marriage and children for the first time in his life. The angel in his dream had awakened in him the desire to make the decisions about his life that God apparently wanted him to make, and to be the man God wanted him to be.

Through the prayers of the people at the mission as well as his own renewed desires, Elden's life has been miraculously turned around. He is now married to a fine musician and they have two children—the very boy and girl he dreamed of.

Elden Lawrence's experience was also unique in that he saw in his dream an angel who looked like an angel. In most of the first-person accounts I have heard, this is the exception rather than the rule. Usually the angel who delivers a message looks like an ordinary person, and it is only after the visit that the person realizes he has been ministered to in a gap experience by an angel.

There was no visible evidence that distinguished the angel who spoke with Mark Buntain in the airplane over India from any other passenger—until he disappeared. But there were any number of unusual things about the visit John Weaver had with an angel, yet at the time it all struck him as perfectly normal.

While John was pastoring a church in Bozeman, Montana, he learned that a group was being organized in the vicinity to try to disprove the virgin birth of Jesus and to discredit the Bible.

Some men in the group were ordained ministers who carried a lot of influence.

John himself had worked hard to establish a church and to uphold the truth; and his congregation had been planning to build a new worship hall. But now he feared his parishioners would suffer as the local group worked to undermine orthodox Christian teaching.

Needing time away to think and pray, John took a few days off to hunt elk in Wyoming. One morning while hunting just below the timberline, he enjoyed a beautiful sunrise on the deep snowy slopes. He was praying, asking God to remove his fear of the future and help his church raise the money they needed, when he looked up to see another hunter emerge from the timberline and begin moving toward him. Within minutes the hunter closed the distance in long, smooth strides, sat down casually on a stump and gave John a friendly greeting.

"Sure is beautiful around here, isn't it?" said John.

"It sure is. But if you think it's beautiful here, you should see where I just came from—," and he went on to describe the glories of heaven.

As the visitor talked, John had an odd feeling he knew him from someplace. And for some reason he couldn't quite explain, he found himself opening up to the stranger, explaining about his church back in Bozeman and the new group in town and even his congregation's new building project.

"How much money do you need to finish the project?"

"Twenty thousand dollars."

"Don't be afraid to take your stand for what is right," the hunter said emphatically, "and don't be fearful about the future of your ministry or your church. The money will come." Then, without another word, he rose, strode back up the hill with amazing speed, and disappeared into the trees.

Looking after him in surprise, John felt grateful that such a friendly stranger had spotted him in the wilds of Wyoming and gone out of his way to encourage him. The more he thought about it, however, the more puzzled he became. How could this hunter have known of the beauties of heaven, which almost had to be what he had been describing? And how could he have spoken with such reassuring authority about what was to happen at John's church?

Not only that, but the more John thought about it, the more he realized the man had covered the distance to and from the timberline faster than anyone on foot could have done. Still staring in the direction the man had disappeared, John noticed the most amazing thing of all: he had left no tracks in the snow!

Suddenly John's memory was jogged. It had been thirty years before, in the summer of 1953, when he left for Bible college. His old car had broken down along the way, and he thought he was stranded until he noticed a man in a brand-new car driving across a plowed field directly toward him.

As soon as he arrived, the man seemed to take charge. Somehow he knew before John had a chance to tell him that John had been considering trying to locate an old friend who lived in a city nearby. He drove John straight to his friend's house, where he was able to afford a car the friend happened to have for sale, and continue on his way to Bible school.

It was an odd experience he had never been able to explain. Now John knew that, even though his eyes had been shielded while the hunter was with him, this was the same angel of the Lord once again, sent this time to exhort him to be courageous.

His apprehension disappeared and John Weaver returned home, where all the pieces seemed to fall into place. The group of dissenters did not hamper his ability to minister, and he soon received two checks for the building project from unsolicited donors totalling twenty thousand dollars.

Knowing of these miraculous events, can we possibly believe that angels are no longer dispatched to deliver messages to God's people today?

An even more astonishing account of a messenger angel's visit, if that is possible, comes from my brother Marvin. Maybe it was the same angel who had quietly protected him when the radiator cap blew off in his face. But there was nothing secret about this second visit.

Marvin told me how discouragement had settled on him and his wife, Sharon, because of some family goals and plans they did not seem to be reaching—for either themselves or their two children. In some ways spiritually, they almost seemed to be stagnating.

One night Marvin felt particularly frustrated, not knowing just what to do. He prayed for about an hour and then went to bed, falling into a deep sleep almost immediately. Hours later he dreamed about some of his family's problems that, in the dream, were resolved amid God's rich assurances.

Whether from the dream or from the power of the Holy Spirit surrounding them, Marvin and Sharon awoke together and were amazed to see the room as bright as if it were midday. At the side of the bed stood an angel, huge and glowing. The angel leaned over and grasped both of my brother's hands in one of his large hands, saturating his body with the power of God.

Marvin told me he felt something like a strange heat, cool and yet white-hot, in his hands and burning in his chest. He felt utterly weak, overwhelmed by the indescribable power in the room. Outwardly he felt paralyzed; inwardly he felt as light as dust dancing in bright sunshine. Then he registered a mental telegram: "Fear not, little flock; for it is your Father's good pleasure to give you the kingdom" (Luke 12:32, KJV).

In another moment the angel folded Marvin's hands together and vanished, right before Marvin's eyes. The room was cast into the pitch black of night.

Marvin's eyes struggled to refocus. His breathing was labored; his chest and hands still burned with that strange, cool fire. Then life flooded back into him with a dazzling flow of energy.

Could the experience actually have been real? As

an inquiring, speculative sort of person, he wondered if the experience had just been part of his dream. But, as if in answer to his question, his spirit reacted like a cage full of fluttering doves—a resurgence that confirmed to him the reality of the visit.

It was then he remembered Sharon, who was sitting quietly beside him. He was about to confirm that she had witnessed exactly what he had, when he felt something in his hands where the angel had folded them together. He reached for a flashlight by the bed and shone the beam on the object in his hand. To his surprise, it was one of the Scripture cards from their "promise box," a little box they kept on the windowsill above the kitchen sink. Neither he nor Sharon had carried the little card upstairs, yet there it was in his hand.

Excitedly Marvin read aloud the verse on the card. It was the same one the angel had spoken to him in the thought language: "Fear not, little flock; for it is your Father's good pleasure to give you the kingdom."

Sharon was as transfixed as he was, and as convinced of the reality of their heavenly visitor. But as the days passed, both hesitated to share the experience with anyone else—until amazing things began to happen. In the following weeks they discovered a church they felt was the Lord's provision. Marvin received an unexpected promotion in his job. New opportunities in the community opened for the children. All four members of the family enjoyed new opportunities to share their faith in God, and were able to pray with people who came to them looking for answers. All of these helped to bring about the goals that Marvin and Sharon had had for their family. It had indeed been God's good pleasure to give them the Kingdom.

Perhaps not all angelic visits are as striking and overwhelming as the one my brother told me about, but the message will come across nonetheless. However God chooses to communicate, He will do so clearly and understandably. Whether by a revelation from the Holy Spirit or by a surprise visit from an angel, God will reveal the answers to our questions in the gap of indecision.

Nor does it matter whether we know that the visitor is an angel. There seem to be three kinds of angelic visits: when we sense at the time that an angel is with us; when we realize later that an angel has come; and when we never do have any idea an angel has ministered to us. With regard to this latter kind of angelic visitation, I have often wondered how many times a casual word from a stranger might have been more than that. Perhaps it was angel guiding, protecting, or relaying a message meant to encourage or point us in the right direction.

I am struck by a fascinating verse from one of the Psalms that may offer a couple of clues about messenger angels: "For thou hast made [mankind] a little lower than the angels" (Psalm 8:5, KJV). Does this mean that until we join the hosts of heaven ourselves, by the death of our physical bodies and the inheritance of our new eternal bodies, that the angels in service to God are of a little higher rank than we are? Apparently so. It may also mean they are more powerful physically, and capable of doing many things we are not, like traveling to and from the throne room of God and riding the winds of heaven.

We know from Scripture that the angels rejoice when a sinner repents (Luke 15:10), and through their obedience to God, they are actually working for the day when we believers will be in heaven and no longer "a little lower" than they. Their selflessness is an important factor in our accepting their messages when we are caught in the gap of indecision.

That selflessness is also one big difference I have found between the angels who continue to serve the Lord and those cast out of heaven because of their pride and lust for power. Those fallen angels or demons are constantly working against us and against the power of the Lord's hosts. They hope to turn us from our commitment to serve Him. We must be careful, then, that we are hearing one of God's own representatives before we follow any message, for the evil one is full of temptations.

Temptations are common to everyone. It is helpful to understand where they come from and what help we have against them.

Take comfort. Satan, or Lucifer, and one-third of the angels were cast from heaven. That leaves us with a two-thirds majority of good angels working for us!

ANGELS AND TEMPTATION

In our struggle to live Christian lives, we are constantly battling evil and fighting temptation. Just as Satan tempted Jesus when He walked on earth, so he tries to block our service and commitment to God. Most of the time we know right from wrong, and all too often we would rather give in to temptation than resist it.

There are two forces at work, one for us and one against us, both of which we shall look at in the course of this chapter. We also have to contend with our own sinful natures, of course, which struggle for their own way. Remember Jesus' admonition to "watch and pray so that you will not fall into temptation" (Matthew 26:41). And keep in mind the help that we as believers have at our disposal.

Fern Backer, who lived a mile down the road

from us, learned a little about this help firsthand
through an encounter with a silent angel while she
struggled with a severe temptation.

Years before she had battled an alcohol problem,
but through the patience of a loving husband and
praying friends, God performed a miracle. She was
delivered from alcoholism and was living a victori-
ous Christian life.

Then one of her sons joined the "wrong crowd."
He started drinking heavily and acting destructive-
ly. Fern knew he had stolen some equipment and
destroyed some more that belonged to a nearby
school. When he was arrested and a trial was
scheduled, it nearly broke her heart.

The day her son was to appear in court, Fern sat
on the couch at home, hardly able to withstand the
stress. One temptation was to fall apart emotional-
ly. Another was to lean on her old crutch: Alcohol
would surely drown her sensitivity and carry her
through a difficult moment.

Fern sat for a long time with her eye on the
outside door, lingering in a gap of temptation.
Should she walk out that door, get into her car, and
purchase a bottle?

She looked steadily ahead, then blinked hard. For
a moment she thought her eyes must be playing a
trick on her. It looked as if a bright light was
dancing between her and that door. Out of the light
a figure formed, a shape that turned into a large
angel clad in white. He did not speak, but his
powerful supportive presence and the look on his
face let Fern know without a word that she did not
need a drink, and that all would be well.

The angel left silently, the light fading to normal daylight hues. For a long time she remained motionless, absorbing the strength and courage her visitor had generated. She chose not to go out for a drink.

Her son, as it turned out, fared well in the trial, which marked the beginning of a new maturity for him. And Fern, for her part, is grateful she held firm against the temptation of alcohol, and knows she is being strengthened day by day.

When Jesus faced temptation in the Garden of Gethsemane, He prayed that the cup of suffering and death would pass Him by, but added a statement that shows His perfect obedience to God the Father: "However, not my will but thine be done" (Matthew 26:39). He was saying, in effect, "Lord, I want to go one way, but You want Me to go another. I'll go the way You want." After His prayer, an angel was dispatched from heaven to help Jesus face what seemed impossibly difficult.

Notice here that Jesus knew His Father's will when He said, "Thy will be done," and He prayed for the strength to follow it. This is a wise form for us to follow too. When we pray we should ask the Lord to reveal His will to us and then pray accordingly, act obediently, and wait patiently.

If an angel ministered to Jesus, and Jesus tells us that we will do greater things than He (see John 14:12), then we too can expect angels to help us stand firm when temptation comes.

Phil and Mavis Church faced a kind of temptation different from the physical pull of alcohol that

Fern Backer fought. Theirs was a temptation to doubt the goodness and healing power of Jesus that they believed were theirs to claim as Christians. The difficulties came with the birth of their third child.

When little Jennifer Rose was born, her parents were filled with joy and gratitude to God for entrusting them with a new little life. But their happiness soon took on an edge of fear. When she was just two days old, the doctor detected a certain abnormality in her physical responses. He ordered tests immediately, and stunned the parents by reporting "positive" results: mental retardation was likely, in addition to a number of possible physical disorders.

Test followed test in order to diagnose Jennifer's condition, and by the time she was four months old, having spent much of her short life in the hospital, her little body was sore from the probing needles. She also showed a fear of strangers.

Phil and Mavis Church clung to their belief that Jesus conquered pain and sickness by His death on the cross. But a temptation began to seep into their thoughts and conversation: the temptation to doubt that God could heal this little child, and even that He was caring properly for her. It was especially difficult to keep hoping in God's care when each day seemed to bring more symptoms and more devastating news.

At six months Jennifer was tested for cerebral palsy; then she began having violent seizures. After weeks of praying and hanging on to the thinning threads of hope, Phil and Mavis checked Jennifer into another medical center for days of specialized testing, thinking their situation could hardly get much worse.

But it did. Doctors broke the news to them one Saturday morning, when the Churches had left their two older daughters with a sitter all day, that Jennifer had a tumor on her brain that had to be removed immediately. The operation itself was risky, but without it she would certainly die. They had little choice but to consent to the operation. Surgery was scheduled for the following Tuesday morning.

Then, in what seemed an unusual move, the doctors agreed to let the parents take Jennifer home for the weekend, so the whole family could be together. "But be careful," warned one of the doctors. "One blow on the head could possibly end her life."

Heavy-hearted, Phil and Mavis barely spoke during the few hours it took to drive home. Once there, they settled Jennifer into her crib, where she was cooed to through the bars by her two sisters. Then the tired and concerned parents went into their bedroom and dropped to their knees together in prayer. The temptation to doubt that Jesus would or could heal Jennifer was almost over-whelming. But once more, resolutely, they offered themselves and their child to His care.

As they continued to pray, they heard a knock at the door. Mavis got up to answer it, with Phil intending to head into Jennifer's room to check on the girls. But through the glass storm door they both saw an unshaven old man in tattered clothes standing on the porch.

They exchanged glances. This was a stranger, after all, and how could they handle anyone else's problem right now? But sympathy must have won out for the sad look on the old man's face, because Mavis opened the door.

"Could I have something to eat, please?" he asked. "If you could give me something, I'll sweep your porch for you."

Mavis glanced at Phil, then nodded. Phil joined the old man out on the porch while Mavis went to the kitchen to fix some food. The conversation soon turned to to the foremost subject on Phil's mind—Jennifer's illness. And as Mavis came out and placed a tray with a sandwich and cold drink on the small porch table, Phil was explaining about the tumor and the operation their little one faced on Tuesday.

The old man's eyes filled with tears, the food seemingly forgotten. "May I see her?" he asked.

Phil hesitated. Besides, Jennifer was afraid of strangers. But something in the man's appeal caused Phil to nod and lead the way to the crib.

Jennifer was still the object of the doting attention of her two older sisters, but as soon as she saw the old man she smiled and reached out her hands to him. Phil started to speak, to tell the man not to lift her for fear the child's head would be bumped, but for some unknown reason he kept quiet. The old man leaned down and lifted Jennifer up gently, cradling her and talking to her softly. Then he put a wrinkled hand on her head and said, "Little angel, you will not have to have surgery, for there is no longer anything wrong with you." Then he smiled at Jennifer and put a nickel into her tiny fist.

He handed the child to her father, turned, and walked out the door.

For a moment the young parents stared at each other. Then they heard the storm door swung shut. Mavis hurried to the door and looked out. There was no sign of the man, and the sandwich remained untouched where she had put it on the table.

That night they all marveled over how peacefully Jennifer slept, and the contentment she showed all day Sunday. Only on Monday morning did Phil and Mavis feel the familiar stabs of fear, the temptation to despair.

They made the long drive to the medical center, entrusted Jennifer to the doctors, and awaited the results of the final examination and X-ray prior to surgery the following day, almost afraid to breathe.

They did not have to wait long. Soon two doctors appeared, shaking their heads and looking puzzled. "We can't explain it," said one, "but the X-rays show no sign of the tumor."

"We don't know what happened," added the second doctor, "but we would like to keep her here for a couple of days just to make sure she's all right."

In the days that followed, the doctors affirmed their new findings. They handed Jennifer once more to her parents, but this time with a smile and assurances that "she's fine."

That ride home was a celebration. Joy swelled in their hearts as Phil and Mavis each thanked God for fulfilling His promises and remaining true to His Word. And that night before they tucked each of their three healthy children into bed, Phil opened his Bible and read aloud: "Let brotherly love continue. Be not forgetful to entertain strangers: for thereby some have entertained angels unawares" (Hebrews 13:1–2, KJV).

Jennifer was indeed fine. She is now ten years old, a healthy little girl in every way. She enjoys telling her friends about her healing and she echoes her parents belief: "I met an angel of the Lord!"

As always in the gap of temptation, the responsibility for the choice is ours. Phil and Mavis could have allowed discouragement, even believing a lie about God's healing power and loving care, to rule their minds. But they chose instead with God's help to maintain their hope and faith.

We have no way of knowing what would have happened to Jennifer had they given up. But since an angel ministered to Jesus in the Garden of Gethsemane *after* He relinquished His own will (Luke 22:43), I wonder if when we choose the wrong way we hinder angels' ministry in our lives. We might be throwing roadblocks in their path by willfully surrendering to temptation.

Not that we don't get plenty of outside encouragement to surrender to temptation! There is a counter-force at work as we walk through life—the force for evil. There are not only good angels available to help us in the gap of temptation, but there are evil angels, or demons, working to influence our moral choices.

When Satan, formerly the magnificent angel Lucifer, was cast out of heaven, he took a third of the angels with him. Even though that still leaves a two-thirds majority of the Lord's angels fighting battles for us, outnumbering Satan's forces two to one, we need to heighten our awareness of the one-third that fell and of their demonic activity.

Scripture tells us clearly that these spirits have been actively fighting against God from the time they were expelled from His presence. Look at two of Satan's disguises: "Your enemy the devil prowls around like a roaring lion looking for someone to devour" (1 Peter 5:8), and, "Satan himself masquerades as an angel of light" (2 Corinthians 11:14). He and his demons lurk full of plans to tempt God's people into rebellion.

Evil spirits were depicted in classical mythology as sirens, sorceresses who sang to the sailors in their ships and lured them to their deaths on the rocky coasts. With their seductive singing, the sirens tempted the sailors, inflaming their passions, playing on their lusts and carnal appetites, until the mariners were "drugged" into submission.

The lure of sin is like a drug of drowsiness to the spirit, making us willing to overlook the consequences of our actions. The longer we continue in a sin, moreover, the harder it is to awaken from it.

Temptation, the counterfeit of goodness, comes with seductive ways and a song. If temptation did not sing or look like an angel, it would have no power to entice and beguile. Evil with its mask torn off, its ghastly deformities and ugliness naked and exposed, would cast no spell. But because we are entranced by its allure and seeming harmlessness, we let the evil ones close enough to clutch us by the throat.

How vital it is that we recognize our freedom as God's children to choose rightly! For us the sirens of sin can sing in vain. We can sail a straight course into the arms of Jesus.

I love the little chorus we sing at church based on 1 John 4:4: "Greater is he that is in you, than he that is in the world." The reason we can sing that chorus is that Jesus defeated Satan by dying on the cross and rising again. This victory enabled Jesus to say, "Take heart! I have overcome the world" (John 16:33).

Satan cannot stand before the blood of Jesus that lost him the battle. For this reason demons—and even certain people—cannot stand to hear mention of the blood of Jesus, the substance absolutely critical to our atonement from sin. Many times during temptation or fear I have spoken aloud the fact that Jesus' blood "covers" me and protects me. No demon can stand against that, no matter how hard he tries to get me to succumb.

Demons' primary focus is to keep men from the saving grace of Jesus. To do this they will deceive believers into accepting distortions of the truth. Let me show you what I mean.

An acquaintance of mine had impressed me as being a sincere and dedicated Christian. When she found out I was interested in the subject of angels, she made a point to come and tell me about her special angel, "David." As she talked, her story struck me as a bit suspicious, as though she enjoyed an ongoing intimate relationship with a spiritual being. When I asked her who this David was, I got a surprising answer.

"Oh, you know him quite well," she responded, and went on to describe the lad centuries ago who slew the giant Goliath and reigned as king over the nation of Israel. She believed David was her guardian angel and that David's son Solomon was her daughter's guardian angel, and she urged me to find a "medium" through which I, too, could receive important information from David.

This was clearly deception. God absolutely forbids His children to consult mediums or spiritists or anyone who consults the dead (Deuteronomy 18:11–12). In Israel in Old Testament times, the penalty for dealing with the occult was death. King Saul, under strong judgment from God, took his own life the day after he used the witch of Endor to conjure the spirit of Samuel.

This acquaintance of mine, far from communicating with David, as she supposed, was listening to a spirit, a counterfeit posing as David. Suffice it to say that her spiritual perception became distorted and her life a tangled mess. The voice she trusted to give her important information only led her deeper into darkness.

Another individual who became deeply involved with the spirit world exemplifies what happens when people seek the companionship of demons.

This woman I know reacted to severe family problems by withdrawing. She soon became alienated from anyone outside her own family. She trusted no one. Frantic with fear for herself and her husband and children, this woman turned (with their approval) to a "spiritual advisor" for counsel. The advisor told her not to worry; that each member of her family would now have a guardian angel for protection.

Soon these "guardian angels," actually demons, came on the scene, but rather than protect the family from supposed dangers, they filled their lives with terror. One demon, for instance, would appear as a little girl and run through the house screaming. Others took the forms of snakes and slithered into their rooms.

There seemed to be no escape. The woman even turned to drugs and alcohol to escape the reality of what had formerly seemed unreal. Even moving to another home did not drive the spirits away.

Happily for this family, they were reached with the gospel and committed their lives to Jesus. Only then did the frightening apparitions leave.

In some cases spirits do not give up so easily. They may mock and impart the message that there is no use trying to be rid of them. In these cases, a victim can speak the name of Jesus, plead Jesus' blood, and quote the Word of God, as well as be freed from these spirits through the ministry of deliverance that Jesus Himself practiced and imparted to His disciples. The evil ones cannot withstand the weapons of our warfare, which the apostle Paul talks about in 2 Corinthians 10:3–4, for those weapons "have divine power to demolish strongholds."

Demons do not attack only those involved in some kind of evil, such as consulting a spiritual medium. Someone very close to me, a dedicated Christian and prayer warrior, experienced a direct spiritual attack as Satan apparently hoped to turn him from his Christian duties.

One evening he spent hours in prayer, and decided to continue praying in the solitude of his church. He used his key to unlock the front door and after entering the church building, he locked the front door again and went into the sanctuary, closing the vestibule doors behind him.

After a long time of prayer at the altar, he heard the heavy front door open and close. He assumed that the minister, who lived next door, had seen the light, noticed the car outside, and had come to pray with him. When the sanctuary doors opened he looked up and expected to see the minister, but they were already closing with no one in sight. So he assumed the minister had peeked in, been assured that everything was fine, and slipped back out, not wishing to disturb him.

Expecting to hear the front door open and close again any second, he resumed his praying. Instead he heard footsteps approaching.

He looked around again but saw no one. Puzzled, he resumed his prayer, until he heard the footsteps for the second time, and the sound of a heavy individual seating himself on the front pew. Not to be outdone by eerie-sounding noises, my friend began to pray aloud, and then was astonished to hear the "individual" rise and to feel cold breath blowing across his face and neck. When he looked up, something grasped his throat and began to grapple with him physically, all the while permeating him with intense cold.

My friend gasped the name *Jesus,* whereupon his adversary immediately released him, as though he had received a blow, and fled from the church.

This incredible account demonstrates dramatically why it is so vital that we do not look to any source but Jesus. Angels can point us *to* the way, but only Jesus *is* the way. If God chooses to send an angel to help us, then that angel will acknowledge Jesus as the Son of God, and will give us direction absolutely in keeping with the teachings of the Bible. Don't be afraid to ask Jesus for discernment.

If one in the guise of an angel comes with direction or a message and ninety-nine percent of it sounds feasible, reject it all on account of the faulty one percent. It is interesting to note in this regard that D-Con is not all poison; it is mostly edible grain. But the small percentage of poison is strong enough to kill the vermin that eat it.

It seems, then, that we have abundant help in refusing temptation, as well as the strength to help us once the decision is made. We know that the Bible strictly forbids any involvement with the occult. We can call on the name of Jesus for protection. And His angels will fight for us and strengthen us.

8

THE RIGHT
APPROACH

It is vitally important to keep our thinking on angels in the right perspective. We need to remember two important points, which we will consider in turn: First, we are to look only to Jesus for help, and never to the angels themselves, just as the angels look only to Jesus for direction. And second, both angels and humans share a common mission—to worship only Jesus.

The apostle Peter explained that "Jesus . . . has gone into heaven and is at God's right hand—with angels, authorities and powers in submission to him" (1 Peter 3:22). Although it is permissible for us to seek angelic assistance, there is clearly only one right approach—through Jesus Christ.

When Jesus was resurrected from the dead and ascended to the throne room of the Father, He became our Intercessor. He knows our needs, prays

for us day and night, and—as the 1 Peter passage
makes clear—commands many regiments of ministering angels in response to our prayers. As we pray
according to His will, He places our requests before
the Father, then orders them into action.

Angelic forces answer our prayers upon Jesus'
command, not ours. We must go through the
proper channels, and we must maintain the proper
attitude before God. After all, even Jesus subordi-
nated Himself voluntarily to the Father.

When He allowed Himself to be arrested, for
example, He told His disciples: "Do you think I
cannot call on my Father, and he will at once put at
my disposal more than twelve legions of angels?"
(Matthew 26:53). So if Jesus submitted Himself in
this way, we too need to submit ourselves to God
and express to Him our need.

Unfortunately, we do not always follow Jesus'
example. At other times, when we do make specific
requests of God, we ask amiss, as James wrote,
because we approach God "with wrong motives"
(James 4:3).

Does asking for personal help constitute wrong
motives? I don't think so. Our heavenly Father
cares for us and is concerned over the most intimate
details of our lives.

David Roever learned just how concerned God is.
When he was in Vietnam half of his face was blown
off by a grenade and he had to be transported to a
hospital in the States. Before his wife could get
there, she feared he might be so discouraged he
would try to take his life. "Lord, preserve him until

I get there," she prayed. "Let Your angels prevent him from taking his own life."

Perhaps it was divinely inspired intuition, for she was right. While she was praying for an angel to surround and protect him, David somehow got a mirror, and felt so hopeless on seeing his reflection that he reached over to pull the tube that provided him with oxygen. When his wife arrived, however, she found him still breathing but hungry. He had mistakenly pulled the tube to his intravenous feeding.

David Roever's life since then has not been easy, of course. He had to undergo convalescence and reconstructive surgery. But his wife was at his side to support him, and they are both grateful God answered her prayer and sent an angel to intervene in what otherwise would have ended his life.

David's wife went directly to God with her request. And her request was not a selfish one. God does indeed want to help His children, right down to the smallest details.

Once when my husband took a bus ride through Bangalore, India, he watched as a native woman carrying a heavy basket on her head boarded the bus. She sat down with a furrowed brow and a frown, still carrying her burden on her head.

The driver of the bus looked in the rear view mirror and called out, "Ama"—meaning *Mother*— "set your basket on the floor and let the bus carry it for you."

She responded with a look of mixed relief and embarrassment and put her heavy bundle down.

There was no need for the woman to carry her load when the bus could carry it for her. Nor is there any need for us to take on physical or spiritual burdens that God wants to carry for us. How many times have we blocked the protection of our guardian angels—who are part of God's care for us—simply because we refused to throw our burden on Jesus? As we have been exhorted: "Cast all your anxiety on him because he cares for you" (1 Peter 5:7).

Even so, God often acts on our behalf in spite of us, just as He sometimes takes the part of loving Father toward those who are not yet His children.

I received this letter from a young woman who was brought to salvation because of angelic activity in her life:

Dear Betty,

Before I knew anything about angels, I fell backward on some ice and I felt two huge warm hands under me. I did not even hit the ice; I was just laid down gently. I saw nothing. At that time I thought I was saved, but God knew I was doubting Him and He had to get my attention. He did. Now I believe positively. I've learned about angels since then. Thank God this experience brought me to Jesus and salvation.

> Your friend,
> Genevieve Hanson
> Spokane, Washington

Despite the compassionate or powerful ways God

can use angels in our lives, however, we need to be careful not to give credit to the angels themselves, but only to God. Angels were created to serve and worship God (Hebrews 1:6–7), not to be worshiped themselves. When the apostle John was visited by an angel on the isle of Patmos who came to reveal events to come, he was so awed he fell down to worship at the angel's feet. "Do not do it!" the angel warned him. "I am a fellow servant with you.... Worship God" (Revelation 22:8–9). And Paul includes angel worship as sufficient to "disqualify you for the prize" of eternal life (Colossians 2:18).

Scripture states clearly that it is wrong to worship angels, although we can respect their work as servants. They are commissioned by Jesus to provide us with courage, healing, protection, comfort, and other kinds of miraculous intervention. But angels' multiple and profound ministries always point toward Jesus, carrying His word to His people and returning the glory to Him.

Perhaps if we could keep the ministry of angels in the right perspective, rather than either sensationalizing it or else refusing to acknowledge its validity at all, the Lord would let us see even more of their activities.

Even so, He does entrust us every so often with incredible evidence. By this I mean the phenomenal photographic records of angelic appearances. Though these are ultimately unprovable, they may provide fascinating glimpses into the supernatural realm.

The first of three of these glimpses was given to me by a friend in Flasher, North Dakota. While a keen photographer friend of hers was in Italy, he shot some unusual cloud formations with the aid of a powerful lens. The picture is amazing, even shocking. In the color photograph, the sky is brilliant with amber tones and dazzling rays of yellow light. Beams shoot upward, much like the prayers ascending from the earth to the throne room that I saw during my death experience.

There are also what appear to be two rows of angels standing in horseshoe-fashion as if they are facing a throne. As they wait at attention, their arms are lifted in awesome choreography worshiping Jesus.

The photographer believes these are actual "prayer shafts" as described in Revelation: "Another angel, who had a golden censer, came and stood at the altar. He was given much incense to offer, with the prayers of all the saints, on the golden altar before the throne. The smoke of the incense, together with the prayers of the saints, went up before God from the angel's hand" (Revelation 8:3–4).

Another friend gave me an unusual photograph taken by neighbors of hers, a young couple, during their first airline flight. They were apprehensive, but their friends and relatives assured them that angels protect the airways when Christians pray. Once on board, they relaxed and enjoyed the first half-hour of the trip, watching the clouds and taking almost a full roll of film to capture their beauty. Then the captain announced they were heading into some unexpected turbulence. The plane began to lurch and drop in terrifying motions, while the couple prayed, amazed at their calm. Then they passed through it and landed safely.

Once home, they picked up the developed prints and stared unbelieving at one of the photos. There in a cloud formation was what looked like a huge angel with a confident expression and arms outstretched, as if commanding safety.

In a third example, I have a phenomenal tape recording of a small congregation in London, England, singing the familiar Gaither chorus "Alleluia." As the people repeated the song several times, they felt a divine response to their worship, as though God had accepted their praise and was pleased. Gradually, they realized, the song had grown in fullness, volume, and range: they were being accompanied by a massive choir!

After the service they replayed the tape. Recorded on it was the mysterious choir, singing in sustained tones leaving no breaks for breathing, and voices far out of human range. A music teacher found that the highest notes were two octaves above middle C, as well as the A above that, getting near the top of the piano register.

Each of these examples would invite more suspicion if the photographers or church congregation had been out to record some supernatural happening. None of them was. But how could such miraculous events possibly be captured by the human instruments of tape recorder and camera lens? I have always believed that if you can explain it, it is not a miracle. We know that, on occasion, God can and does open our spiritual eyes and ears so that we can see beyond the "normal" realities of our world. Can He not open the eye of a camera lens as well? And if He chooses, can He not allow us an early sampling of the sounds of "Home"—the voices of countless angels joined, as they will be someday, with the church's praise and worship of Jesus?

The important thing to remember for now is that in every miraculous event surrounding angels, we should focus on Jesus. They carry out His commands, give Him glory, or tell others of His comfort and love. No matter how thrilling an angelic visit may be, we are to keep our eyes on Jesus, approaching Him in prayer concerning His angels, and worshiping Him only.

9

CLOSING
THE GAP

There is much we can learn from angels, those tireless servants of God. For God has called us, too, to minister to His children in the gaps they face: to help others in their stand against evil; to encourage those facing indecision to understand God's direction and feel assured in His care; to help the helpless, hungry, poor, sick; to strengthen those fighting temptation to stay in the will of the Lord; and to intercede for the needs of others. Most important of all, we are to declare to a lost world that Jesus is Savior.

This is where angels excel. They are servants, ambassadors, agents, and interveners working to protect the eternal soul from damnation, from the everlasting gap of separation from God. In the fields outside Bethlehem they announced Jesus as the Savior of the world, and we can join the heavenly hosts in reaching the people of every nation with the Good News.

A fascinating testimony from a Japanese woman named Constance reveals how our work and that of angels can blend in an person's life to bring him or her to salvation.

Constance had accidentally fallen into a river in Tokyo and was drowning. As she struggled frantically to keep her head above water, yet began to sink below the surface for the fourth time, she knew she could not survive any longer. Then, unaccountably, she described how "strong hands" came up behind her and carried her to a shallow place along the shore. Finally able to stand, she turned, gasping and shaken, to thank her rescuer, but no one was there.

After that mysterious deliverance, Constance determined to find God. On January 1, 1954, she wrote in her diary: "This is the year I must find true God. It exists. I will find it." The next day she saw a poster inviting any who were interested to come and hear an American missionary couple. Hoping they could help with some of her questions, she attended the meeting and was amazed that they had no images of gods on the wall. The Japanese, as Constance explains, have eight million gods, everything from fish heads to hawks.

She described this new Christian faith like this: "They worshiped an invisible God who must be like the angel who had rescued me from drowning in the river—unseen. Their God was inside each one of them, and He transmitted out of them to me as they told of it, and sang about it. The missionary said, 'Jesus is the Prince of Peace, the forever joy that doesn't depend on outward circumstance.' I went forward to find Him and His peace. I said, 'My heart witnesses missionary tells truth.'"

Constance learned later that the couple had been praying for an interpreter for their meetings. Though at first they were disheartened that she was their only convert, they rejoiced to learn that she was a school teacher and eager to help them.

Constance knew her family would feel betrayed by her new beliefs and try to compel her to revert to their paganism. Sure enough, within a few days a family gathering was planned, and Constance realized her new belief—or her life—was at stake. She prayed that God would reveal Himself to her at that moment as the only God, or she could not face the difficulties ahead.

"Suddenly," she said, "I speak in English, in Japanese, then in a different language. I knew then that if the whole world say, 'He is not God,' I will know He *is* good God."

When she first arrived at the family celebration, she was unable to speak in any but the new language. Her father and brother, the "family lords," took her to a room, shut the door, and tried to "beat and kick Jesus out of me." But she felt no pain, only a holy Presence. She was ready to die for the true God; death would only mean the ecstasy of seeing Him.

The men continued the beating until her mother broke into the room and threw herself across her daughter's body to save her. Disgusted, they left, and Constance was able to escape to the missionaries' home.

Sometime after this, she read in her Bible that God's angels are "ministering spirits sent to serve those who will inherit salvation" (Hebrews 1:14). Because of an angel's service to her, rescuing her from the river, Constance had been introduced to Jesus and inherited salvation. She realized that God had been seeking her all along and had put the desire in her own heart to seek Him.

Several years later, solid in her Christian faith, Constance was thrilled to take her eighty-five-year-old mother, who had suffered a stroke, to a church meeting where she met Jesus and received Communion. She was healed in soul and body.

Through the prayers and work of two missionaries, as well as one strong angel, Constance had been saved and equipped to minister to others. She and her American husband, now missionaries to Japan, tell others the truth of the gospel, and still testify how angels protect us so that we might be saved and invest ourselves in the salvation of others around the world.

Similarly, a group of Christians in Indonesia, who were trying to reach the lost, made a discovery about the close involvement of angels. They were constructing a church building, but had only limited funds. So they decided to take a photograph of the unfinished church and send copies out with the request for money to complete the work.

When the pictures were developed, however, the

negatives were blank. Then someone remembered they had not prayed before the photo session, and suggested they try again by asking the Lord to be in charge of the picture and the request.

In the second set of pictures, to their astonishment, a tall angel could be seen standing in the door of the unfinished building, as though welcoming visitors and supporting the project.

After that, all the funds they needed showed up. And once the building was constructed, the revival fires burned and many searching hearts found the way to Jesus. The Indonesian Christians realized it must have been an angel of salvation endorsing a "soul-saving" station.

My friend Morris Plotts, himself a prayer warrior, related a third account showing the lengths to which angels will go to bring the gospel message to those in need of it, and how we ourselves can actually take something of the role of an angel. It is so miraculous that I hesitate to include it in this book. I have written it in, then taken it out again, no fewer than four times! Even though the story is hard to believe, however, I do believe my friend Morris implicitly, and have finally decided to share it with you, too. It happened to a missionary friend of his.

Ernest Bruckman had been interceding for hours at a time daily that unbelievers in Russia would come to the joyous knowledge of Jesus' saving power. Besides praying, he had sent written materials and tape recordings, all in Russian, to help those in home Bible studies to spread the gospel.

One night after prayer and fasting, Ernest looked up to see an enormous angel standing before him, who spoke these few words: "I have a mission today for you." Ernest found himself being transported faster than the wind, then walking down a path in a strange city. He passed a vegetable garden and saw a house at the end of the street. He walked to the door, quietly pushed it open, and walked into a small gathering of people huddled over a tape recorder.

They looked up with smiles as though they knew him and were glad to see him. One of the men spoke to him in English: "This is your testimony, Mr. Bruckman. We've been praying that you would come here to teach us more."

Ernest talked with them hours and hours, until he was spent. They asked questions and soaked in all of his words as though they were parched and he held their only refreshment. Finally they shared a meal with him, which consisted of a crude, hardened black bread. It left a sawdust-like residue in Ernest's mouth, so he ate slowly, holding the small loaf in his hand, not wanting to refuse their generosity.

Then without warning he felt his body being transported again. He found himself in his own home, still chewing the hard bread, with his astonished wife staring from his face to the black loaf in his hand. He related his incredible experience and put the loaf on a shelf in the open cupboard as a reminder to continue his prayers.

A few days later a friend of Ernest's came by to

see him, and noticed the bread. He recognized it as the homemade black bread he had seen being made during a previous trip to Russia. He was planning to go again, and Ernest described for him as well as he could the location, the road, the house, and the name of the group, all of which he had learned in his long hours with them. The friend promised to do his best to find them.

For weeks Ernest waited anxiously for his friend to return from his trip, although somehow he suspected he would find the group. Even so, Ernest was amazed all over again to hear his friend describe the location and people he had seen during his strange trip. His friend said the group told him of the night "the preacher" came, and the many results accomplished because of his ministry.

When my friend Morris told me this story, I had to be honest with him. "Morris, this is pretty hard to understand. Do you believe it really happened?"

He responded by reaching for his Bible. Morris is nearly eighty years old and still does mission work in Africa where he has built several churches and schools. He opened his Bible to Acts 8:26–40 and began to read aloud:

> Now an angel of the Lord said to Philip, "Go south to the road—the desert road—that goes down from Jerusalem to Gaza." So he started out, and on his way he met an Ethiopian eunuch, an important official in charge of all the treasury of Candace, queen of the Ethiopians. This man had gone to Jerusalem to worship, and on his way home was sitting in his chariot reading the book of Isaiah the prophet. The

Spirit told Philip, "Go to that chariot and stay near it."

Then Philip ran up to the chariot and heard the man reading Isaiah the prophet. "Do you understand what you are reading?" Philip asked.

"How can I," he said, "unless someone explains it to me?" So he invited Philip to come up and sit with him.

The eunuch was reading this passage of Scripture:
"He was led like a sheep to the slaughter,
and as a lamb before the shearer is silent,
so he did not open his mouth.
In his humiliation he was deprived of justice.
Who can speak of his descendants?
For his life was taken from the earth."

The eunuch asked Philip, "Tell me, please, who is the prophet talking about, himself or someone else?" Then Philip began with that very passage of Scripture and told him the good news about Jesus.

I nodded as Morris continued reading the familiar account from Acts. I, too, was beginning to understand.

As they traveled along the road, they came to some water and the eunuch said, "Look, here is water. Why shouldn't I be baptized?" And he ordered the chariot to stop. Then both Philip and the eunuch went down into the water and Philip baptized him. When they came up out of the water, the Spirit of the Lord suddenly took Philip away, and the eunuch did not see him again, but went on his way rejoicing. Philip, however, appeared at Azotus and traveled about, preaching the gospel in all the towns until he reached Caesarea.

Then Morris closed his Bible. "This story of Philip shows the Lord's diversity," he said slowly. "He can easily give a word of direction for us to follow, so that, like Philip, we can walk directly to the person in need. But, again like Philip, the Lord might miraculously transport us wherever He wants us. Philip was transported to preach. Why not this man of God who has interceded for the Russian people for so long? God works in a mysterious way."

I had to admit he was right there. God's ways are certainly beyond my limited understanding. It would be wrong for me to doubt God's abilities just because I found the miraculous hard to believe.

Yet aren't most of God's dealings hard to believe? Who can understand such a heart of forgiveness as He has? How can we begin to comprehend the love that would allow His own Son to suffer and die so that we might be able to live forever with Him? It is the same loving and compassionate heart that continues to hear our prayers and send us help, and who created the angels to minister to those who will inherit salvation.

Perhaps we question the ministry of angels because we have not experienced the same thing. In John 12:28–29, when a voice from heaven spoke to Jesus, we are told that some said it thundered while others said an angel spoke to Him. Yet John and presumably others clearly heard a voice speaking.

Since not all heard the same thing, does that invalidate the experience?

The Lord has many ways of reaching us, His ministering angels not the least. They watch over us tirelessly, helping us over gaps that at times would overcome us, pointing us always to Jesus.

Angels are watching over you and me, until the happy day they can usher us into the throne room of the mighty King—what the black poet James Weldon Johnson called "that great gettin' up morning." And there together we will worship Jesus forever.

EPILOGUE:
A LOOK AHEAD

God often does the extraordinary through the ordinary. It seems that His mysteries are revealed more fully through the simple and trusting hearts that walk with Him every day. Jesus once prayed, "I praise you, Father, Lord of heaven and earth, because you have hidden these things from the wise and learned, and revealed them to little children" (Luke 10:21). He meant in part that sometimes we know with our hearts what our minds cannot comprehend.

Jesus is seeking believers, ordinary Christians like you and me through whom He can remove fear, reveal His hope, and display a new dimension of love, especially in these troubling days when despair has settled over so many hearts.

It seems we are living in a time that parallels the events in the book of Acts, waiting for the events of the Revelation. We have witnessed Jesus among us and are commissioned to spread the good news, but we have not reached the time when Jesus returns for His own. And just as it seems our ability is accelerating to reach the far corners of the earth with the gospel, opposition to that message may be raging as never before.

Satan does not simply want to keep us from telling others about Jesus. He wants those of us who know Jesus to turn from Him. Personally, I think Satan would like to blow up the earth. That would not only kill all believers but stop the Word from reaching anyone else through them. That thought might be very frightening, considering there is enough power in the hands of men right now to destroy this planet, except for one thing—God's holy angels.

The apostle John, seeing the earth through spiritual telescopic vision, said: "I saw four angels at the four corners of the earth" (Revelation 7:1).

Now, consider what we have learned about the earth from science. The Bible does not say that the earth is square, but that there are four corners—four bulges, if you will. When astronaut Ed White and his crew photographed the earth from the vantage point of outer space, their pictures showed four distinct bulges in the earth. The first is from the north of Ireland to the North Pole; the second is from South Africa to the Antarctic; the third is from the islands of New Guinea to Japan; and the fourth is about two hundred miles west of Peru.

The angels stationed at these four corners, as I

see it, are holding back winds of destruction, the power to harm the land and the sea. Angels not only have that authority, but I believe they will someday bind Satan and cast him into the lake of fire, where he will be tormented with other deceivers forever (see Revelation 20:10).

I am anticipating that day when "the Lord himself will come down from heaven, with a loud command, with the voice of the archangel and with the trumpet call of God, and the dead in Christ will rise first. After that, we who are still alive and are left will be caught up with them in the clouds to meet the Lord in the air. And so we will be with the Lord forever" (1 Thessalonians 4:16-17).

He is counting on us to get a lot done before He comes again. It may mean walking by faith rather than by sight—but then, we have the encouragement of knowing that a great angelic host is helping us every step of the way.

MY GLIMPSE OF ETERNITY

MY GLIMPSE OF ETERNITY

BETTY MALZ

Chosen Books

A Division of Baker Book House Co
Grand Rapids, Michigan 49516

ISBN 0-8007-9066-9

ISBN 1-56865-152-X

This book is dedicated to

everyone who needs a miracle

ACKNOWLEDGMENTS

To Len LeSourd for the months of hard work and professional "know how" he invested . . . taking my raw material and refining it into digestible reading. His shepherding and tutoring has been to me a journalism course I could not have afforded.

To Catherine Marshall for her "reader's digest form" of my story that got my writing career "off the ground" ("A Glimpse of Eternity," May 1976 of *Guideposts*).

To Carl, my husband, for keeping his hand in the middle of my back, sometimes patting, sometimes pushing.

To my gracious mother-in-law, Dorothy Upchurch . . . for her patience with me during the long years of my immaturity, and for allowing me to express and confess about *us*.

CONTENTS

CONTENTS

INTRODUCTION

My first knowledge of Betty Malz came through a pamphlet mailed to me by a stranger. The story it contained riveted my attention. Betty's experience seemed like nothing so much as a modern version of the raising of Jairus' daughter (Mark 5:22–24; 35–43); it was so spectacular that it defied credibility. I knew then that I would have to investigate it all the way.

Correspondence with Mrs. Malz eventually resulted in a date set for a visit with us at Evergreen Farm in Virginia. "May I bring my daughter April with me?" she wrote.

A few days later as the passengers from Houston streamed through the gates at Dulles International Airport, Len and I immediately spotted Mrs. Malz and her daughter. Tall and willowy-slim, clear eyes in a face alive with the joy of life, Betty is still a young and attractive woman. The delightful nine-year-old with long blonde hair two steps ahead of her mother opened with, "Do you have any horses on your farm?"

Laughingly, her mother explained, "April has a passion for all animals. She wants to be a veterinarian when she grows up."

Later that evening, while April was outside happily making friends with Toby and Gretchen, the two dogs, and Spooky, the cat, her mother settled down to talk. And then I heard from Betty's own lips the story of her amazing experience.

It happened when she was twenty-seven years old. In the Union Hospital of Terre Haute, Indiana at 5 A.M. on a July morning, 1959, Betty was pronounced dead, a sheet pulled over her head. The Lord had awakened her father, the Rev. Glenn Perkins, at 3:30 that morning and had told him to take the forty-minute drive back to the hospital. It was part of God's master plan that Betty's father was to be standing by his daughter's bed to see for himself the drama about to take place.

In *My Glimpse of Eternity*, Betty Malz describes her experience on the other side of that dividing line that we call "death," then how she returned to her body on the hospital bed—to the stunned amazement of her grieving father and the hospital personnel.

"You make dying sound like good news," her husband John later told her after listening to her experience.

This book *is* good news for all of us whose mortality haunts us.

Upon occasion God breaks into human life to give us a glimpse of what lies ahead for us. Betty Malz's remarkable experience is a resounding "Yes, there *is* life after death." More than that, "Yes, God is real and does, in our time, still have power over life and death."

Yet *My Glimpse of Eternity* is even more than that. For

it is the story of how God dealt with a proud, materialistic, controlling woman who had to die to learn how to live.

Here is a ringingly triumphant book, a love letter from the Lord of glory to each one of us.

CATHERINE MARSHALL

Evergreen Farm
July 5, 1977

PROLOGUE

THE TRANSITION was serene and peaceful. I was walking up a beautiful green hill. It was steep, but my leg motion was effortless and a deep ecstasy flooded my body. I looked down. I seemed to be barefoot, but the complete outer shape of my body was a blur and colorless. Yet I was walking on grass, the most vivid shade of green I had ever seen. Each blade was perhaps one inch long, the texture like fine velvet; every blade was alive and moving. As the bottoms of my feet touched the grass, something alive in the grass was transmitted up through my whole body with each step I took.

"Can this be death?" I wondered. If so, I certainly had nothing to fear. There was no darkness, no uncertainty, only a change in location and a total sense of well-being.

All around me was a magnificent deep blue sky, unobscured by clouds. Looking about, I realized that there was no road or path. Yet I seemed to know where to go.

Then I realized I was not walking alone. To the left, and

a little behind me, strode a tall, masculine-looking figure in a robe. I wondered if he were an angel and tried to see if he had wings. But he was facing me and I could not see his back. I sensed, however, that he could go anywhere he wanted and very quickly.

We did not speak to each other. Somehow it didn't seem necessary, for we were both going in the same direction. Then I became aware that he was not a stranger. He knew me and I felt a strange kinship with him. Where had we met? Had we always known each other? It seemed we had. Where were we now going . . . ?

MY
GLIMPSE
OF
ETERNITY

1

THE WARNING

THROUGH THE HALL window I saw my mother-in-law walking up to the front door, suitcase in hand. With a low moan I realized that John had done it again. He had invited his mother for a visit and had forgotten to tell me.

It could not have come at a worse time. John, our daughter Brenda and I were getting ready to go on vacation. Drawing a deep breath, I opened the door with a smile of welcome.

Mother Upchurch dropped her suitcase on the hall rug and looked around. There was severity in the way her jet-black hair was done up in a bun on the back of her head. The strong set of her jaw was somehow heightened by the mole in the middle of her chin. Her probing dark brown eyes mirrored a sharp and active mind.

"New drapes?" she asked, pointing to the living room.

I nodded and braced myself for the question I knew was coming.

Dorothy walked into the living room and studied the

drapes for a moment before slipping behind the long daven-port to feel their texture. "They go well with the furniture," she said, approvingly, as she studied the red, white and black color motif of the room. "How much did they cost?"

I sighed. "Less than you would believe." Then I turned the conversation to something else, irritated that I had to give so many evasive answers to her questions about how much John and I were spending on our possessions. My replies ranged from a terse "not much" to "about half of what it was worth" to "an unbelievable bargain."

Sensing my annoyance, Dorothy retrieved her suitcase and quickly headed for the guest bedroom where she always stayed, leaving me to fight down my guilt feelings. Dorothy Upchurch, despite her probing manner and unannounced visits, was not a selfish person. Her appearance in the home of her children always meant pans of fresh cookies, succulent baked dishes, washing, mending, ironing—the giving of herself to dozens of small tasks. She deeply cared for the members of her family. If only she weren't so efficient and so often right in her observations and evaluations.

Later that afternoon, before John came home from work and Brenda returned from a playmate's house, Mother revealed her primary concern as we sat drinking coffee at the kitchen table.

"John is working too hard," she began.

"John has always worked hard," I replied. "No one can slow him down."

"You can," she said, her intense eyes drilling holes through me.

It was a tired, familiar conversation. John had been sick with rheumatic fever as a boy. A heart murmur resulted but doctors couldn't agree as to whether there was heart damage, or if so how much. Meanwhile, John had grown up intensely competitive in athletics, an outdoor man who loved hard work as the manager of a Sunoco service station in our home town of Terre Haute, Indiana.

Dorothy sipped her coffee and kept her eyes on me. "The work he does at the station doesn't worry me so much as the financial pressure he's under," she continued.

"What financial pressure?" I asked, fighting down irritation.

"The pressure to pay for a new car, a new boat, and now I understand you're thinking of building a new home," she said.

I bit my lip to keep from lashing out at my mother-in-law. Why did she meddle so much in our affairs? Emotions under control, I tried to explain that we were not reckless spenders, that John knew how to manage money.

But Dorothy doggedly returned to the issue of her son's health. "I know in my spirit that John will have a heart problem unless you slow him down," she said, her lips tightly pursed together.

Dorothy made her visit a short one when she learned we were getting ready to go on a vacation. Her concern for John's health nagged at me for several days until I firmly decided that my mother-in-law was a negative thinker about her son. I was not going to dwell on death, but life. At twenty-nine, John's vitality seemed endless. We loved sunshine, water, boats, convertibles, tennis, music. At twenty-seven, I felt so glowing with good health that I could not recall being sick in bed for even one day of my life.

And yet my physical death was only weeks away!

The morning before we were to leave for our two-weeks'

Florida vacation, my husband began the day on the run as usual. Still buttoning his shirt, John slid into the turquoise leather breakfast bar of our kitchen and ordered "one glass of orange juice to match the wall." I had just finished painting the kitchen wild tangerine.

As I set the juice in front of him, John impulsively leaned his head against my side, then squeezed me, his muscular arms around my waist. His affection had always been as spontaneous and impulsive as a child. When he released me I served him his coffee and scrambled eggs and bacon. Then I brought over my pot of tea, a cup and saucer and slid in beside him.

"Look at the label on this tea bag," I said. " 'Discontent breeds progress.' That describes me, John. I've been restless for months, but getting ready for this Florida trip has cured me."

John's face clouded. "The vacation is off, Bets. I just can't leave the station now."

He couldn't be serious, I thought to myself. I searched his face. It was sober and boyish, his pug nose dotted with freckles, but the amiable lightheartedness was gone. I had sensed a heaviness in him when he came home from work the previous night. Obviously not wanting a before-bedtime confrontation, he had waited until now to hand out the bad news.

"Why are you doing this to us?" I asked stonily.

"The new foreman isn't ready to handle things on his own and Ike's been gone for two days," he replied. "Our help situation is a mess."

"Ike is the problem," I snapped. "You've got to fire him. He only cares about two things—pork chops and Sweet Lucy (wine)." All my pent-up hostility toward black people poured out in those words.

"Ike is a good mechanic. I can't fire him just because he has a problem with Sweet Lucy," John replied evenly.

"Somewhere there must be another good mechanic you could hire," I said crossly.

John just shook his head. "It isn't only the problems at the station. We're loaded with debts and the vacation will only put us in deeper." He finished his breakfast quickly, gave me a peck on the cheek instead of the usual lingering kiss and charged out of the house. The zoom of the engine, the grind of gears, as he sped to work were just a few tell-tale signs of my husband's mad dash through life. "Jittery John" my mother called him. She would warn him that life was meant to be sipped, not gulped. John would just smile at her.

He was also inclined to think out loud. My parents, Glenn and Fern Perkins, had asked us to dinner several weeks before. While we were talking about our proposed Florida vacation at the table, John suddenly blurted out, "Come along with us. Dad, you can drive the boat while Betty and I water-ski. Brenda and Gary can play together, and Mother, think of the rest you will get under the warm Florida sun."

Although our two families got along very well, I wasn't certain that I wanted to spend a two-weeks' vacation with my parents. But as we talked my enthusiasm grew. Our daughter Brenda was six years old. My parents' last child, Gary, was also a six-year-old. When Mother and I were both obviously pregnant, we had embarrassed my brother Jim by sitting side by side wearing maternity dresses at his high school graduation. My baby was born first, so Mother took care of me and Brenda when I came out of the hospital. In return, five weeks later, I ministered to the needs of Mother and baby Gary. Not every mother can have a daughter and a brother so near the same age—who enjoy playing together as they grow up. Over the years Mother had become a kind of insurance policy during family get-togethers. She watched the children closely and was in constant prayer for the safety of all of us when we were around boats or traveling in the car.

As I washed the breakfast dishes and cleaned up the kitchen, I decided not to call my parents just yet with the news that John had cancelled our vacation. Perhaps he would change his mind again. I focused my thoughts on that probability. Prayer, to me, was the heart's desire put into words. "Lord, You know how much I want to go to Florida," I prayed softly.

There was more to this trip for me than just a Florida vacation. I was bored with our life in Terre Haute. Our comfortable ranch house, the convertible, the yellow and white cabin cruiser which we kept at nearby Lake Catarack —all things we had worked hard for—had somehow not brought us fulfillment. A change of location was needed, I had decided. And Florida had the answers for both John and me. A gasoline station in the travel-heavy vacation state would be ideal for my husband. With his drive, John could quickly develop it into an all-purpose automotive business, as he was doing in Terre Haute. For me, the year-round outdoor life would be a true answer to prayer. Expenses would be less too. No worry about winter coats and boots.

The morning's setbacks and irritations continued. Brenda awoke tired and cross; at the breakfast table she overturned a glass of milk. When I found a moment to relax and turned on the radio, the music that poured forth made me cringe. Oh no! It was Art Lindsey's program. The way this free-lance preacher scrambled together country western music with religion was enough to ruin your day.

I suppose that part of my annoyance was caused by the way Art sauntered into our church on Sunday evenings and accompanied the song service with his guitar. We liked the way we had always handled this part of the program through organ music. Art was always putting the emphasis on praise. "Let everyone that hath breath, praise the Lord," he would say, quoting Scripture. Then he would suggest songs that were folksy and not in keeping with the mood of the service.

I snapped off the radio and put on my favorite Jack Holcomb record; Holcomb's singing of the great old hymns fed me more than almost any sermon.

I went down the hall to make the beds and glanced with a pang at the matching mother and daughter swimsuits I had laid out to pack. They were yellow and white-checked gingham with a ruffle on the bottom of the short skirt; Brenda's had several rows of ruffles covering the seat section which she labeled her "bimer." The ruffle helped to hide my too-thin figure. I winced at the memory of myself at age thirteen standing five foot nine inches tall and weighing but 100 pounds. My brothers used to say, "We never believed that storks delivered babies until Betty was born. Most kids look like their parents, she looks like the stork." To offset my self-centeredness about my skinniness, I became an energetic doer, proud of my good health and school accomplishments in music, drama and academics. Learning that tall women rarely get sympathy because they never seem to appear as if they require it, I took pride in my independent attitude.

The thought spell was broken by the phone ringing. I wanted it to be John with good news—and it was. "Have you called your folks yet?" he began. "Good. This new man is working out fine and Ike is back on the job. The guys want me to take this vacation and they say they'll work extra hours if necessary. Let's take some money out of savings and leave tomorrow as planned. You need it; I need it. I can feel the tug of the tow rope, the spray in my face, and the sand between my toes already!"

His exuberant voice set my heart to singing. My dream was going to come true, all of it. There was only the faintest negative thought in the far reaches of my mind—a tiny inner premonition that I determinedly ignored.

The next morning, John and I were at the breakfast table when Brenda bounced through the door. "I'm all ready. I did my own packing," she announced proudly. She stood there with her long blonde curls, wide blue eyes and glowing pink cheeks. She was dressed in a blouse and ruffled panties, but no skirt. In her hand was a round pink plastic suitcase which she called her "suitbucket."

It's a good thing I decided to examine it. Out jumped her little black and white kitten "Pumpkin Face," named for his round countenance and entrance into the world on Halloween. Also tucked inside were her swimsuit, sunglasses, a red Delicious apple and four pieces of bubble gum.

"What will you sleep in?" I smiled at the absence of any night clothes.

"In our motel, of course, Mommie."

Dad and Mom and Gary arrived soon after breakfast. With careful planning we had decided that all six of us could fit fairly comfortably in our spacious Pontiac. Now came that frantic last-minute packing and closing up of the house. My dad put his car in our garage and began fitting luggage into the trunk of our convertible. Calm and unflappable at fifty, Dad's quietspoken wisdom and unselfish

24

strength fed both his family and a congregation of 300 he pastored thirty-one miles to the south. Dad loved the outdoors, whether it was hunting, fishing, boating or gardening. His gear always included a Bible, a concordance and clipboard for making sermon notes.

In contrast, my forty-six-year-old mother, Fern Burns Perkins, was a worrier. A descendant of poet Robert Burns, she had inherited some of his gift for verse, but took her homemaking role with total seriousness. Mother loved to bake and sew and keep an orderly house. During my school years I recall getting off the bus only twice when she wasn't there to meet me. Once she was in labor at the hospital having my third brother, Marvin; the other time she couldn't get home from shopping because a freight train was stuck for forty minutes at the crossing.

Her last son, Gary, taxed her patience to the limit. Adventuresome, with mischievous blue eyes, Gary had broken both arms in different escapades in the four-month period before our vacation trip. Once after a visit to the circus he tried unsuccessfully to tightrope-walk on the backyard clothes line. The other break came when he attempted an acrobatic flip over the round leather hassock in our living room. Arms now mended, he jumped out of the car, grabbed Brenda's hand and raced her to our backyard swing, an automobile tire hanging on a rope from the limb of our sycamore tree.

John was on the phone with last-minute instructions to his shop when I realized we had made no arrangements to have our family collie and kitten fed while we were gone. "You and your animals, Betty," was John's only comment when he heard my dilemma. Dogs and kittens had been a long tradition in our family. My grandmother, whom everyone called Mom Burns, told me once that my mother had twenty-two assorted animals at one period when she was a child.

I had just finished working out a plan for a neighbor to feed our animals when Mother came in the house, an exasperated look in her eyes. "Gary and Brenda have gotten filthy on that swing," she reported.

With one final flurry of energy on that warm June day in 1959, we closed and locked all the windows, turned off the water, left a note for the milkman, another note for the paperboy, said goodbye twice to the animals, brushed the dirt off Gary and Brenda, made three last-minute trips into the house to retrieve a jacket, a baseball glove and a piece of mosquito netting. I leaned back exhausted on the rear seat of the car as Dad drove out the driveway.

The adults may have been worn out, but the children certainly were not. Brenda, on my left, stood upon the floorboard behind the driver with her little arms wrapped around her grandfather's neck, tight enough to choke him. "This is my Papaw," she cried.

Uncle Gary, five weeks her junior, had been looking out the window on my right. Quickly he took exception. "This is no Papaw; this is my daddy," he shouted, pulling her away. Sitting between the two contestants, I began to wonder how much vacation there would be for us.

For John and I greatly needed it. My husband had worked day and night for months to make a success of his business. The vacation would help relax his frayed nerves. As for me, I was in a deep rut and desperately wanted a change. I felt I had been a good mother, wife, Sunday School teacher, church organist and neighbor. Working so hard to make a good impression on others had deeply drained me. What was wrong? Why did there seem to be so little real joy in all my strivings and achievements?

For a moment I was envious of my father who received such deep satisfactions from his faith. How did he do it? He went about things so calmly, almost effortlessly. Just the way he was driving now, relaxed, serene, at peace with himself and others. When prodded about his serenity, Dad would smile and say that all peace and power come from Jesus. The answer seemed so pat.

We ate dinner somewhere near Chattanooga, Tennessee, and decided not to stop for the night until we were well into the state of Georgia. John was driving and I was sitting in front with him and Brenda, who soon fell asleep against my side. As the car grew quiet I continued my musing. John could find a new business opportunity in Florida. It was such a logical move for an outdoor family. Our plans to build a new home in Terre Haute could be adjusted to the Florida terrain. Even Mother and Dad might want to move down and join us.

Brenda, as she slept, seemed a bit heavy leaning against my right side. I shifted her slightly, but the discomfort in my side remained. I shook it off and closed my eyes to dream about our future life in Florida.

2

NIGHT EMERGENCY

CRYSTAL INN is located twenty miles north of Clearwater, Florida—an unspoiled, lovely cypress lodge on the rim of the Gulf of Mexico and part of the Gulf Vista Retreat Center. The six of us were the only guests, taking over all the upstairs rooms where we could see the waves roll in. Our view was unhindered except for one spot in the center—an aged banyan tree, gnarled, with heavy waxed foliage, writhing in and out of the earth.

Much of our first vacation day was spent on the sunporch resting and listening to the rustling sound of palm fronds in the breeze and the lapping of the waves on the shore. The sand was the texture and color of fine white bleached cake flour; the water was crystal-clear.

The high point of the day was to see Brenda's face as she caught her first fish, just four and a half inches long, and pulled it out of the water. It was too small to eat, but she would not throw it back. She insisted she was going to take it to Indiana in the trunk of the car to show her other grandparents.

Gary had been entranced by the beach, too, especially the fiddler crabs. We spent an hour trying to teach him to float on his back in the water, but he had trouble relaxing. Irrepressible Gary never seemed to stop moving.

In many ways, my husband John and Gary were alike in their childlike approach to life. While my parents and I had been happy to relax on the sunporch and absorb the fragrances of Florida, John had been in and out of the water, up and down the beach on various investigative sorties, and then instigated a short trip to another island where we watched porpoises play and gathered up sand dollars along the shore.

One discordant episode occurred when John brought us the local afternoon newspaper. On the front page was a story about a young boy who had drowned nearby in the ocean. Mom sucked in her breath and vowed even closer supervision of Gary and Brenda. I found the story of this death a jarring and unpleasant note. It reminded me of my recent conversation with Dorothy Upchurch and her fears for John.

In the evening as the sun sank below the water, soft organ music began drifting out over the Gulf. It came from the steeple of an old church of Spanish structure, dull yellow stucco in color, nestled among tall stately palms at the end of Crystal Beach Avenue. Out on the water we could see fishermen in shrimp boats cut the motors of their boats to drift and listen. John was enjoying the music too, relaxed for the first time that day.

Amid the tranquillity of the moment, my thoughts returned to the drowning we had read about that afternoon, and then to the only dead person I had ever seen—my tiny two-day-old baby brother.

"Mother, I'd like to ask you a question," I said suddenly. "How did you feel when your baby boy died so soon after his birth?"

My mother looked surprised at the unexpected question. "I grieved to be sure," she said softly, and we were silent for a while reliving that memory. The baby was a breech birth and his tiny spinal cord had snapped in the process. The private family service had been held in the beautiful chapel of a West Terre Haute funeral home. Aged ten at the time, I sat next to Aunt Pearl in a lovely velvet chair, while my little brothers Don and Jim were with Mom Burns nearby. The tiny form lay in a small silvery blue casket banked with rosebuds and baby's breath flowers.

There had been organ music, and the pastor had read from Scripture and spoken a few words. At the close of the service I walked past the open casket and vividly remember how pretty he was—dark brown wavy hair, round face with olive skin. I did not grieve. I had not known him and felt no particular need for him since I already had two little brothers that I loved dearly.

"Grief can get to be very self-centered," Mother continued. "I soon realized that some day we would see our son in Heaven and that he would not have a severed spinal cord, but would be perfect and happy and so glad to see us. There would be a most joyful reunion."

"You make death sound like such a happy event," I said unconvinced.

"I believe that it is," Mother said while Dad nodded vigorously.

My doubts were obvious and I did not pursue the subject. Death was the end of life as I knew it. How could that be good news? John, too, was uncomfortable. If anything, he loathed the subject of death more than I did.

I snuggled up to my husband and reached for his hand. John's intensity had always attracted me. He had always reached out for life. It carried over into every area: work, play, love-making, and lately the church where he had begun energetically leading group-singing. In his early teens John and his two younger brothers had provided the main help for the family tomato farm in Middletown, Indiana. At fifteen John dreamed of owning a fancy car. By the time he had a driver's license he had worked so hard and saved so much he was able to buy a used Cadillac convertible and thus became the envy of his schoolmates.

Then came a period of youthful wildness which brought him close to death on two occasions. Once while driving a gravel truck at work, he overturned it on a slope and he and the truck tumbled into sixty-five feet of water. The water pressure made it impossible to open either the door or roll down the window. Somehow with his last breath he broke the window and swam to the top.

One night while driving home after a drinking party, several boys in the car with him dared John to try and beat a train to the railroad crossing. Forgetting the freezing road conditions, John gunned the engine, hit an icy spot and the car skidded into the moving train. John was the only one badly hurt, suffering a broken leg and bad cuts on his head and cheek.

I first met him one Sunday shortly after this mishap. He was on crutches and had beamed a lopsided grin in my direction, looking a bit comical with his bandaged head. I learned later that he had refused to go out with his crowd the night before, stating, "I'm going to church in the morning. I hear the new minister has a pretty daughter." They had just hooted at him.

31

That Sunday morning, he really did look as if he had been hit by a train. I saw a battered youth one inch smaller than me and was not a bit impressed, because I was looking for a tall sophisticated young man with polished charm and spiritual depth.

How grossly I underestimated John's drive and determination! He went home that Sunday and told his mother and dad that he was going to marry the preacher's daughter. John then left his wild crowd, entered into church activities and became a warmhearted, loving and unselfish person, winning my heart in the process. We were married two years later at Thanksgiving.

John had been working in the heat treat department of a New Castle, Indiana, automobile assembly plant. His job was to take 90-pound axles and stick them into a blast furnace for tempering—a physically demanding task. Soon after our marriage, I persuaded him to move to Terre Haute where John became manager of the Sunoco service station at the corner of Ft. Harrison Road and Lafayette Avenue. Johnny's Sunoco Corner soon expanded to eight pumps, a car wash, a tire and battery business and then a used car lot. Always the materialistic dreamer, I foresaw a series of service stations for John, who would then move into an executive's role.

Despite his drive John had an impractical side, such as his disconcerting habit of giving credit to poor risks. Poverty-stricken travelers from the south (Kentucky hillbillies) coming north on Highway 41 to Chicago looking for work would stop and were soon telling John their hard-luck stories. My husband would often refuse to take their money, insisting they pay him by mail when they found work. Sometimes they sent the money, sometimes not. I recall one bearded little man who sent us a dollar a week for almost a year to pay for a set of tires.

There were times when John's generous nature made me want to hug him—such as when he would take out his own handkerchief to wipe a child's runny nose, or gently steer a youngster into the washroom, or give a free soda to some tired and impoverished traveler. Then there were occasions when his tenderheartedness made me want to throw a bucket of water on him, like that hectic day before Christmas one year when he arrived home in the middle of the day with a carful of children. I was supposed to babysit while their weary parents went shopping for presents.

My biggest problem after our marriage had been with his mother. I sensed Mother Upchurch's disapproval of me from the start and was always on the defensive. John was most unaware of the tension that grew between the two women he loved the most. Like his father, Oscar Upchurch, he was easygoing and avoided family confrontations. This came out especially over the issue of which church we should attend.

John had always gone to his family church where the service was dignified and carefully structured. In my denomination there was more freedom of worship and lively singing, sometimes with guitars. After our marriage John became paralyzed with indecision, not wanting to displease either his mother or me. Although a bit disdainful of other churches, I would have gone to his if he had asked me, but for seven months he would not go to church at all. Then one Sunday morning without a word he dressed in his best suit and accompanied me to our church. Later he joined.

My resentment of my mother-in-law often came out in the "pity parties" which the wives of her two other sons occasionally held with me when our husbands were at work. I think deep down we both respected and feared her, but it certainly was not easy to love Mother Upchurch.

Somewhat guiltily I reflected on the way I had distorted the story of John's and my honeymoon trip. Since John could not afford to take me on a honeymoon when we were married, his mother and sister Helen volunteered to accompany us to Niagara Falls. Mrs. Upchurch agreed to pay all the expenses, but I never told this part of the story, nor that John and I drove alone to Niagara Falls while his mother and sister stayed for a visit with a relative in Port Allegheny, Pennsylvania. I had always put the emphasis on the meddlesome mother-in-law angle and cast Mother Upchurch in the role of the heavy as I told how she accompanied us on our honeymoon.

Uneasily I recalled how during her last visit only a few days before Dorothy Upchurch had sensed my restlessness and chided me about it in her incisive manner.

"You must learn to be satisfied with what you have, young lady. It's there in the Bible. Philippians 4:11. *I have learned, in whatever state I am, to be content.* And for you and me that should mean the state of Indiana too," she concluded with surety.

I had stared at her in dismay, wondering how she had so accurately understood my state of mind. And her quote from Philippians was on target. The material things in life often pulled me away from spiritual matters, but for some reason Scripture always spoke to me—and had from the time of my conversion at age thirteen.

Still tired from the long trip from Indiana and groggy from the hot sun, we all retired early. John was instantly asleep while I lay in bed fighting a nagging pain in my side that had begun after dinner. I eased out of bed and went out on the screened balcony, watching the beacon on the lighthouse at the tip of a nearby island. The pain in my side throbbed with each blink. Finally, I went back inside, awoke John and told him I needed a doctor. He was instantly alarmed and roused my parents. Dad and John quickly helped me to the car, leaving Mother with the sleeping children. We decided to head for the small beach hospital at Tarpon Springs, nine miles away, which we had passed on the highway.

As we drove out of Crystal Beach the waving fronds on the Robolina and Saga date palms had lost their lustre. The gnarled old banyan tree reminded me of a stooped old witch. For I was writhing, with so much nausea that I wondered when I would have to ask my dad to stop and let me be sick by the side of the road. In a matter of minutes we pulled up in front of the hospital.

The Tarpon Springs Hospital seemed smaller even than the veterinarian clinic at home. A male attendant quickly approached the car door with a wheelchair. I stepped out and was about to reject it when a wave of weakness made me sink into it gratefully.

Inside, the attendant steered me to the emergency room and helped me onto the examining table. I clenched my fists determined to be stoical, remembering the many times in my childhood when my anemic and usually pregnant mother would be stretched out on the couch in a faint. It always seemed to happen with many members of the family present, and assorted grandmothers and aunts would bend over her with cold cloths for her forehead and rub her wrists to stimulate circulation. Mixed with my love and concern was the suspicion that she somehow enjoyed her misery. As I grew older I was determined never to show this kind of weakness.

Dr. James Thompson, the night doctor on duty, was young and gentle. I decided he was too young and good-looking to be wise. As he applied pressure to my lower right side, the ceiling lights separated into small bright specks, like lighted fish eggs, and I passed out. So much for my vow to be strong and unflinching.

When my eyes began to focus again, the doctor asked a series of questions, then did a urinalysis, a blood test and x-rays. After checking results, he spoke frankly.

"You're in trouble. I'm in trouble. I'm afraid that you have a swollen appendix, ready to burst. The blood test shows an infection. I have only twenty-four beds in this little beach hospital and I have twenty-six patients, two of whom are women in labor. I am the only doctor on duty. Your appendix must be removed immediately, but I cannot do it here."

A hurried call was made to the Morton Plant Hospital in Clearwater, Florida, and arrangements completed for the head surgeon on the staff of that hospital to meet me there and have the operating room ready. Dr. Thompson warned me: "If you get relief, you'll know your appendix has ruptured. Do not be persuaded otherwise. Go through with the operation. You need surgery immediately."

The doctor then gave me a shot to ease the pain. Minutes later the throbbing eased and I felt a kind of euphoria. Everything was going to work out fine, I concluded.

Two ambulance attendants entered the emergency room and began preparing me carefully for the twenty-two-mile ride to the Clearwater hospital. They wrapped the white sheet about me as neatly mitred at the corners as a bride's gift for a wedding shower. Then I was lifted gently and seemed to float into the back of the ambulance, the interior of which was quilted and carpeted, with velvet draperies lining the windows. John sat beside me holding my hand, while Dad drove our car behind the ambulance.

I was still euphoric and yet aware of everything—the rotating red light reflecting through the windows, the screaming siren muted somewhat by the well-insulated interior of the vehicle. We were quiet and very much alone, as the drivers had closed the curtain behind them. John then began philosophizing and continued to do so during the rest of the ride to Clearwater.

"How silly our value system is," he began. "We think that money and what we own are so important until a time like this. So last month Sunoco gave me the 'salesman of the month' award; it seemed so important then, but what good is it now? My mother is right—she told me that if you have the Lord and your health, that's all a marriage really needs. It seemed so simplistic, but she's right, Bets."

A male attendant, a nurse's aide and a registered nurse met us at the emergency entrance of the Clearwater Hospital and wheeled me into the prep room adjoining surgery. The necessary papers were filled out and my side was shaved and painted. Dr. Malcolm White, an older man with a harried look, began to examine me. Finally he removed his glasses, wiped his face with his handkerchief, and with a reassuring smile said, "I'm glad Dr. Thompson was not able to operate on you in his hospital. With all due respect to another doctor, I feel he has made a wrong analysis. It would have unnecessarily ruined a vacation for your two families. You have an internal infection which I think we can clear up with penicillin We'll keep you here for a day or so until the infection is gone and the dizziness subsides. You'll be as good as new!"

This was what we wanted to hear. John and Dad returned to our vacation lodge and I went to sleep, reassured.

But the infection did not clear up. Day after day, the doctors conferred, ran tests and gave me shots of penicillin for the infection. The pain returned. When my temperature began to climb, they called in another specialist in internal medicine. After studying the x-rays, he said, "I feel you may have a tubular pregnancy."

On the seventh day of my stay in the Clearwater Hospital several of the doctors gathered together in my room for an "organ recital"—a review, it seemed, of every part of my lower anatomy. When I protested this, John and my dad intervened to suggest that I be flown back to Indiana and admitted to our local hospital there. The doctors agreed to release me, and hours later I was on a plane with John and Brenda for Terre Haute.

When the plane landed at the Terre Haute airport, I asked John to take me home. He was surprised.

"I thought the doctors told you to check into the hospital as soon as you arrived," he said.

"John, the doctors can't agree on anything about me. Dr. Thompson said one thing, Dr. White something else. They've discussed me endlessly, pawed over me day after day. I'm tired of the whole thing. Let's go home. I'll find a way to clear up the infection." Then I remembered that my parents and Gary were driving back in our car from Florida. "I'll be admitted to the hospital when Mom and Dad get home," I said.

Reluctantly John agreed, on the promise that I would

go to bed. He didn't have to pressure me. I felt terrible. But I had another problem too. In my head. It was pride.

As I look back on that decision, it was completely indefensible. Why did I deliberately disobey the doctor's instructions to enter myself into the hospital? The reason I gave John about the doctors not being able to agree on what was wrong with me was true enough. Yet that didn't get to the real issue.

I realize now that I have always been a person who liked to run things. A fierce dislike of hospitals was being born in me because there I found myself utterly out of control. The patient lies on the high bed like a horizontal department store dummy, made to feel like a thing—a piece of anatomy with problem parts—not like a person at all. Was it false modesty or prudishness that made me shrink from the casual uncovering for breast or vaginal or rectal examinations, the constant chatter about my female trouble at the Clearwater Hospital?

Then too one is always at the mercy of the hospital routine—stick the thermometer in the mouth at 6:00 A.M. . . . wake the patient out of a good sleep . . . slap a washcloth on her face fifteen minutes later . . . leave her sitting on the bedpan for twenty minutes—there is little the patient can do to alter the course of events.

Complaining did little good, I found, and often resulted in poor service and less attention. Trying to talk to the doctors did not help much either. I could see it in their eyes and in their impatience always to be off—*I have the knowledge . . . she has none . . . let her talk a little . . . be kind. . . .*

I kept thinking, "But it's *my* body you doctors are discussing. It's *my* life and *my* future at stake. How can you

39

bypass *me* this way?" As a person I felt kicked into the corner and ignored. So I found the whole hospital system an assault on my personhood.

Oh, I tried to be bright and cheery. I would greet the nurses with warmth and the doctors with open friendliness. I wanted them to think me a good patient. But underneath I was in rebellion, primarily because of a feeling of helplessness. I didn't know then how to handle that.

So by trying to take things in my own hands and refusing to enter the hospital for further treatment, I put myself on a collision course between two forces—my pride and a deadly infection.

3

THE COMFORTER

THREE DAYS LATER I awoke in a panic. I was afire with fever. My body had swelled up like a blimp. I could not move my legs, had no feeling in my hands and could barely get my breath.

"John, wake up, wake up. I'm in trouble." The voice hardly sounded like me. It seemed to be coming from across the room. Then I became almost hysterical when I realized I could not see.

John bounded from bed and dialed my parents. "Pray for Bets; she's much worse. Meet us at the hospital emergency room as soon as you can get there."

Then he was calling the hospital, asking for a surgeon. "This is an emergency!" John said, his voice cracking.

I faded and returned, faded and returned again. Feeling came into my hands; they had been asleep. Vision in my eyes returned slightly, but I could not smell or taste.

John dialed a neighbor who agreed to come right over and stay with Brenda. He dressed quickly, then found a

41

bathrobe for me. I felt his arms under my knees and shoulders just as Brenda came into the room.

I focused my eyes enough to see my daughter standing in the doorway in her pajamas with the pink teddy bears printed on them. Under one arm was "Jingles," her large stuffed donkey; in the other was "Pete," her life-sized stuffed monkey.

"What's wrong with Mommie? She's big enough to walk, Daddy; why are you carrying Mommie?"

"It's all right, dear," I said groggily.

As John carried me to the car, I blacked out. A few minutes later I came to when John sped around a corner, tires squealing. As we pulled up in front of the emergency entrance of Union Hospital, a stream of thoughts seared my consciousness like a lightning bolt. I had been born at this hospital; now I was returning here to die.

The next thing I recall was opening my eyes to blurred lights on the ceiling of the examining room, swirling about like a lake of tiny minnows. A physician was standing over me. My husband, remembering that the last examination in the Florida hospital indicated a possible tubular pregnancy and a dead fetus, had called Dr. Paul Bherne, who was a gynecologist and surgeon.

As I faded in and out of my twilight zone, I recall Dr. Bherne sitting at the right corner of the examining cot, taking a ball-point pen from his pocket and scrawling on the white bed sheet a diagram for my husband. He drew a picture of the womb, the tubes and ovaries. "Her tubular pregnancy took place here," he said, pointing to the right tube. "The fetus has been dead for some time: this explains the gangrenous infection in your wife's bloodstream."

Before I was wheeled to the operating room, I was asked

to sign several papers releasing the hospital of responsibility if anything went wrong during surgery. Because of my blurred vision they were read to me and a nurse helped me sign in the proper place. One of the papers, a copy of which I retained, was titled: "Consent to Operation that Will Result in Sterilization."

> I, the undersigned, a patient in Union Hospital, Terre Haute, Indiana, hereby certify: That I have full knowledge that the nature of the operation to be performed under the direction of Dr. Paul Bherne will result in sterilization; that consent thereto is hereby given voluntarily by me, if competent, and for me by my parents, guardian or best friend, as the case may be, if incompetent for any reason; that the Union Hospital and Dr. Bherne shall in no way be held liable for the resulting sterilization.

Below my signature there was another statement for John to sign:

> I, the spouse of Betty Upchurch, the patient above-mentioned, and knowing the contents and meaning of the above instrument, fully agree, request, consent and advise that said operation be performed.

We were signing away any possibility of adding to our family; yet what choice did we have? How sad that Brenda would never have a brother or sister!

I was rolled to the operating room and placed on the table. Another doctor and an anesthetist joined Dr. Bherne. They gave me a spinal injection, then a shot of sodium pentathol in the right arm, and then the countdown—99, 98, 97. I heard myself complaining that it was too cold on that operating table, that he was cutting me too deep, clear through my back and into the table. Dr. Bherne, speaking to a nurse, said, "I know she can't possibly feel that. More sodium pentathol, please."

I didn't feel anything from then on, but pieces of conversation from the medical men pierced my befogged senses. There were comments about "a huge mass," many technical terms, then before I slipped into deep unconsciousness the words, "I don't see how she can survive this massive gangrenous infection."

In my childhood our family used to hold yearly family picnics outside of Rockville, Indiana, beside the brown, one-lane, 30-foot covered bridge which spanned the Wabash River. The river, although swift-moving through this wooded area, was wide enough and deep enough for swimming. The water was so fresh and pure that we drank it.

My uncles loved to roughhouse with us children at these picnics, particularly Uncle Jesse, whose position as a railroad brakeman earned my deep admiration. Uncle Jesse would pick me up like a sack of potatoes. Then I would squeal with delight as I sailed through the air from one uncle's strong arms to another.

In the recovery room after the operation, as my temperature soared to 105 degrees and the morphine took full effect, I dreamed that once again I was flying through the air from uncle to uncle. Then suddenly the scene changed from the Wabash River to a large city, and some tiny pink men were tossing me from a church steeple to the top of an apartment house to a skyscraper. The dwarfed creatures would scream with laughter each time I would almost fall to the ground. Next I found myself being hurled from one jet plane to another as planes were whizzing about me in all directions. There was a terrible pain in my stomach which got worse each time one of the small creatures touched me.

Was this death, I wondered? The voice in the operating room had said I could not survive the infection, yet how could this be death if I could feel such pain? Then I rallied to sound—it was the voice of Dr. Bherne.

"I have never cut into such a nasty mess in all my eighteen years of practice."

Then I heard my father's voice, but not what he said. Then it was Dr. Bherne talking again:

"Dr. Thompson was right in his diagnosis. There was no tubular pregnancy. It was a ruptured appendix. Why, her appendix burst with such impact that all I found of it were small fragments. I didn't even attempt to remove them. Nor did I try to suture the incision back together again. We will leave it open to drain."

As they talked on I only half heard the words, but my father later gave me the substance of Dr. Bherne's grim prognosis for me. Peritonitis infection had coated all my organs, causing some to disintegrate. "I have seen 200-pound men die with a ruptured appendix and no complications," he told my parents. "Your daughter has carried that mass of infection for eleven days. I'm sure it's now spread all through her body. She's a desperately sick woman."

Since few hospitals had intensive-care units in 1959, arrangements were made for around-the-clock nursing—three nurses a day, eight hours each. A stomach pump, connected by a long tube through my nose, had to be closely monitored so that it was properly irrigated and would thus prevent vomiting and hemorrhaging. My blood pressure, pulse and heartbeat were constantly checked. Dr. Bherne asked my parents to keep an eye on the intravenous feeding process to see that the needle connection into the vein during blood transfusions was kept secure. My veins had not responded fully because of the high fever and high infectious content of my blood. Close relatives could visit me, the doctor said, one or two at a time. Either of my parents or John could remain day and night by my side without restrictions.

I knew that this was an extremely difficult time for John. Hospitals and doctors had always intimidated him. Death was something he would just never talk about. Dad told me later that the sight of my drawn white face after the operation had paralyzed him with fear. For days afterward he would arrive for a visit, pat me softly on the shoulder and then station himself outside, seated on the floor and leaning against the door in an attempt to protect me from visitors. He would sit there for hours at a time, moving only to let nurses, doctors and members of the family enter and leave.

I wanted to comfort John, but was too weak. When he would enter the room and kiss me lightly on the cheek, I could barely open my eyes. I needed him there beside me to tell me his business troubles and report on Brenda. It seemed that everyone decided that because my eyes were closed most of the time, I could neither hear nor see what was going on in the room. In reality, I was intensely aware of what was going on.

While Mother stayed home with Brenda and Gary, Dad Perkins would sit by my bed day and night. At certain periods he would stand beside me and pray. Oh how I remember those prayers! The words were like living water dripping into my veins, a healing balm for a fever-ridden spirit. Dad's prayers were so real, so true, so powerful that they were better than any life-support system. He said things like:

"Lord, we are so weak, but You are strong. How we love You, how we trust You, how completely and totally we depend on You. Betty is Your child, Lord Jesus, and she needs Your love and Your tenderness and Your compassion and Your healing touch. We do not beg for her life for any selfish reason of our own. You loaned her to us for a few years and yet we know she has always belonged to You. Oh how we praise You for Your goodness to us during these years, for the blessings You poured upon us, for Your day-by-day presence in our home. We can sense Your love filling this room now. Thank You, Lord Jesus, for Your comforting Presence."

As the words of my father's prayer sank into my mind, I was suddenly convicted of something. Jesus was very real to Dad. Was He to me? For years I had prayed to Him, sung to Him, quoted Him, but I had to admit that I did not feel close to Jesus.

The fault was obviously mine. I had become too involved with my worldly life and felt no need for Him. Up until now I had never really been sick. My parents and John had provided comfort. Brenda had given me fulfillment as a mother. When on earth, Jesus had responded to the needs of people. Up to this point I had had no needs.

A series of scenes flashed before me. I was thirteen. It was Sunday night and Dad had preached a moving sermon on our need to accept Jesus Christ as Savior. We were to be ready for His Second Coming. No one wanted to be left out of the marvelous life which He promised us in eternity.

We drove home from church that evening through north-east Terre Haute, not far from the Paul Cox airfield. From the window of the car I saw a light in the sky descending toward that small airport. Remembering my father's sermon, I wondered, "Could that be Jesus coming back? Was I ready for Him?"

It was a plane coming in for a landing, but my mind remained stimulated. Later, lying in bed in the darkness of my room that night so many years ago, I found myself repeating the words of a prayer I had stopped saying years before:

> Now I lay me down to sleep;
> I pray the Lord my soul to keep.
> If I should die before I wake,
> I pray the Lord my soul to take.

The third line then began to bother me: "If I should die before I wake. . . ." Could this happen? If so, would I miss out on all that the Bible promised? "I'm not ready to die," I thought to myself.

I jumped out of bed and went to my parents' bedroom door. Their light was out. I knocked anyway. "What is it?" my father asked sleepily.

I was embarrassed, then blurted out the first words that came to mind: "I'm not ready to die."

Instantly both parents were wide awake. In his sensitive spirit, Dad knew exactly what to do. He took me by the hand and he and Mom led me down to the living room.

"Betty, are you ready to commit your life to the Lord Jesus?"

I nodded.

I knelt between my mother and father in front of our three-cushioned brown floral couch, one hand in Dad's, the other in Mother's. "Lord, I accept You as my personal Savior. I surrender my life to You for You to do with it what You will."

Then Dad read me some passages in Scripture where Jesus is talking to Martha just before He raises Lazarus from the dead: "Jesus said to her, *I am the resurrection and the life; he who believes in me, though he die, yet shall he live, and whoever lives and believes in me shall never die*" (John 11:25, 26).

Thirteen years had passed since that night, during which period I had gone to church faithfully and tried to live virtuously. But there in my hospital bed I felt His gentle correction: I had lived by rules, but I did not know Jesus. Therefore I had missed the most important part of the Christian life.

Despite the fever and pain, I was aware of the beginning of a teaching process in my spirit. Something in me had been activated by Dad's prayers; my spirit and God's Spirit were touching. Then a strange thing happened.

For years I had loved the recordings of Jack Holcomb, two in particular: "The Old Account Was Settled Long Ago" and "I Have Been Born Again." While lying so helpless in my hospital bed, I heard the music of these great old hymns and the unforgettable words of the latter:

> My heart glows with rapture,
> My cup runneth o'er,
> Such joy, so transporting,
> I ne'er knew before;
> It flows thro' my soul from God's heavenly store,
> For I have been born again.
>
> I'll sing it, and tell it wherever I go,
> I want all to hear it,

I want all to know,
The joy of salvation
That makes the heart glow,
For I have been born again.

During one period of consciousness, I thanked the nurse for giving me this wonderful background music. She looked at me suspiciously and said there was no music in hospital rooms. How then had I heard it so clearly?

Then two events took place which made me more aware than ever before that the Comforter was with me. The first involved the visit of my mother-in-law.

Mother Upchurch had driven from New Castle, Indiana, some 150 miles across the state. The first time she walked into the hospital room with John, negative vibrations began to flow between us. My eyes were closed, but I could almost see her dark snapping eyes studying me, the life support equipment, the vases of flowers. She clucked sympathetically over me for a few minutes, then seeing that I could not respond, turned her attention to John. The questions began.

Was Brenda receiving good care? Who was looking after the house? Were you eating properly? And getting enough sleep? As the interrogation between mother and son continued I learned that John had been living alone in the house (Brenda was at my parents') and that the kitchen had been full of dirty dishes. John admitted ruefully that he had hired a young girl at a dollar an hour to wash the dishes. It had taken her six hours to do them.

I found myself getting upset at my mother-in-law's concern for John. I was the one near death, not John. It was almost as if the whole situation were my fault and she, Dorothy Upchurch, had to get things back in proper order, which she obviously intended to do, beginning with my kitchen.

Yet as I felt my resentment rising the way it always had when I encountered John's mother, a surprising thing happened. Something cool poured over my agitated spirit to quiet me. Like a refreshing ointment soothes bruised skin, this coolness extinguished the hot feelings within me. Then the words were implanted in my mind: *She has reason to worry about John; but she also loves you and some day you will see her as I do and love her too.*

Then it was as if a section of Scripture moved onto a screen in front of my eyes. The verses seemed to be a part of a long psalm:

> The earth, O Lord, is full of thy steadfast love;
> Teach me thy statutes!
> Thou hast dealt well with thy servant, O Lord,
> According to thy word.
> Teach me good judgment and knowledge,
> For I believe in thy commandments.
> Before I was afflicted I went astray. . . .
> (Psalm 119:64–67)

The words of the last verse seemed to enlarge until it stood out from the others. I began to tremble. *Before I was afflicted I went astray.* The Holy Spirit was showing me something through God's Word: that I had gone astray, that I had many things to make right and not just with my mother-in-law. Then I heard the gentle words: *Those who suffer for Me can minister for Me.*

My second experience of the Presence took place at the end of three tortuous days caused by a blockage in my bowel. Before taking me back to surgery, the doctors decided to relieve my distress with a manual procedure that is acutely uncomfortable and embarrassing. As two nurses with rubber gloves worked on me, I gritted my teeth and thought to myself, "This is the most humiliating experience of my life." And as I reached out for the Comforter, a wonderful change took place inside me.

My pride began to slip away as if I were shedding a frayed old skirt. I forgot that I had a body of different parts, some to be seen, some to be concealed. I became one body, one person, one spirit. And as I reached out for Jesus, He laid His hand on my head with such tenderness that I knew He was seeing me as I really was in the world of Spirit. The pain and discomfort fused into a moment of pure ecstasy.

And then there was a quick vision of how God had originally meant us all to be at our creation. Adam and Eve in the Garden of Eden—happy, carefree, unaware of any knowledge of good and evil, unaware of the need for concealment of anything about their personhood, free and open to God and each other.

At the same time I felt a sudden infilling of my body with what I can only describe as a torrent of love. It was the love of Jesus for me, ministered through two compassionate women. In turn, I had the intense and overwhelming desire to love Christ with all my heart, as well as all of His ministering angels. This joy and love so flooded me that I thought I might burst.

There followed a period of sudden relief from pain as though Jesus were saying, "You see now—you can depend upon me to be with you in your moments of agony and despair."

This was exactly the kind of reassurance I needed to face the days that lay ahead.

4
CAPTIVE LISTENER

TWO DAYS LATER I was wheeled back into the operating room for more surgery. X-rays now showed that the ruptured appendix had caused a telescoping of the bowel and thus a blockage. As during the first operation, doctors and nurses assumed that since I was under anesthesia, I could hear nothing of what was said. And so they spoke quite negatively about my chances for recovery.

I have since learned that other patients have had this same experience. A friend of mine named Ida told me that she had been desperately sick in the hospital several years ago. Thinking her completely unconscious, her two children, a son and a daughter, began arguing over who would get certain items of her estate. It was such an ugly scene that Ida, who heard it all, was spurred on to recovery. "I fooled them two ways," she laughingly told me. "I lived, and then changed my will, leaving everything to my niece."

Even when under deep anesthesia, spoken words seem to be received by the patient's unconscious mind, collected and transferred to the brain in a process little understood. There can be a time lapse of hours, even days, before this translation process occurs and the patient has an awareness of what was said. After both operations I knew by their comments that my doctors considered me a hopeless case. I even recall the jokes about my Florida tan.

The result was a struggle inside me between two forces —a feeling of defeat which said that I might as well give up, and a fighting determination not to quit but to battle back. I resisted defeat, but I can see how some people might not. And I wonder how many unexplainable sudden post-operative deaths have resulted from patients who heard their death warrants under anesthesia and in a state of despair gave up and died.

The problem of negative influences continued in my room for days after the operation. Only family members were allowed to visit me, but I belong to a large family. I've since spent hours reflecting on conversations I heard while seemingly unconscious; I've made notes and pondered the whole subject of how the vibrations, attitudes and dialogue of visitors can poison the atmosphere in a hospital room—or bless it.

Three women dropped in for a visit several days or so after my first operation. I later put down on paper the type of things they said:

"Betty's so young too. I believe twenty-seven."

"That's about the age of Susan. She left a four-year-old girl."

"What happened?"

"Susan was riding the ferris wheel at the circus over in Marshall, Illinois. She fell out. Broke her neck."

"How awful! Had she been drinking?"

"We think so. She and Sam were having problems. Sam's remarried now."

"It didn't take him long."

"Brenda will take Betty's death so hard. She and her mother are very close."

"I don't think John will marry anyone who would mistreat Brenda."

"The husband never knows. He's gone too much. John is at his shop day and night."

At this point I was relieved when the subject was changed to operations; but only for a while.

"I hear that it was a doctor in Florida who messed up Betty's case. He diagnosed it as some kind of malformed pregnancy."

"I would think there would be tests to tell the difference between a pregnancy and appendicitis."

"You would certainly think so."

"If, by some miracle, Betty recovers, she should sue."

"It probably wouldn't do any good."

"I guess not. There was the woman in New Goshen who was sewed up after an operation with a sponge still inside her. She had to go back to the hospital for another operation to get it removed. Some tiny veins started to grow through the sponge."

The women chatted on and on as though they were at a coffee klatsch in one of their homes. When they got up to leave, they stopped a minute by my bed. I'll never forget the brief prayer one said: "Lord, give her a peaceful hour in which to pass."

Another woman came to pray for me. Valerie was from our church and I had worked with her on special youth programs. She stood by my bed and began to weep.

55

"Lord, we want Your will for Betty," she began. Then her voice took on a sepulchral tone. "We all have to die sometime, Lord, and we want to be prepared. We pray that You will spare Betty and let her remain with us. But our life here is so short and Your eternity is so long, so we know it is never right to ask for special favors. Instead, we want to be so totally in Your will that whether we live or die makes no difference . . ."

Valerie's heart was loving and her intention utterly self-less. What she said may have been true enough, but the tone of her voice and her weeping mannerisms told me she believed I was going to die. This left me depressed.

Then there was the young couple who came to see me one evening when I was alone. They stood quietly by the bed for a few moments. I was aware of their presence but did not open my eyes. They sat down and began to talk to each other. The husband began:

"Marge, you've left the newspaper in the driveway for two days now. I've told you about this before. It gives the impression we are away and invites prowlers."

"Well, let's stop the delivery. You can pick up the paper on the way home from the office."

"No. That won't work. Some days I'm not near the news-stand."

"Well, you're as bad as I am. When I drove the kids to camp, I came back to find the mail left in the box for two days. One envelope had come open through the humidity and there was seven dollars in cash inside."

"Marge, I had to be gone part of that time on a trip with George."

"I hear he and his wife are getting a divorce."

"It looks that way. Emily's drinking is driving him up the wall."

"I hear that George is chasing around."

There was a short silence.

"I don't think those rumors are fair to George. He has taken a lot in that marriage." Then followed a quick change of subject. "Let's not stay here long. We've got to stop for gas. I'm on empty now, and I want to work some on the lawn."

"By the way," said Marge, "there was a warning on television that we should not water the lawn. The drought seems to be worse. All of Indiana, Illinois and Ohio are in trouble."

"That's all we need. No water."

The couple got up to leave and I was anguished on the inside. With my high fever I had been craving a drink of water, but because of the stomach pump connected by tube through my nose, I was not allowed any liquids in my mouth. Instead, a nurse would rub ice on my lips. Thus the news of a water shortage suddenly depressed me. Though grateful that they had cared enough to stop by, once again my spirit was disturbed. I was left with the feeling that people had written me off as so hopelessly ill that what they said did not matter.

My father was my anchor during those critical first days of high temperature and unconsciousness. For one stretch of eight days he hardly took time to change clothes as he sat with me day and night. In addition to his prayers, there was one phrase he often used which held me fast to the mooring. He would stand by my bed, touch my hand or arm or place his hand on my forehead and say softly, "Bless the name of Jesus."

The words drifted through my fog of pain and fever like soothing crystals of light, dissolving in my body with a deep healing effect. I had played hundreds of hymns on the organ extolling the name of Jesus, but I never knew the full power in His name until that moment. It was as though Jesus Himself was somehow spreading through my tissues, cleansing the poison, nourishing my blood, strengthening muscles and tendons and protecting the life system of veins and arteries. How I loved to hear my father repeat that phrase: "Bless the name of Jesus."

John was in and out during those days and I could sense his worry and tension. His body could hardly remain still. He could not sit in a chair. My inert form and closed eyes unnerved him. I kept wanting to say, "John, I love you. Relax, just hold my hand and talk to me. I can hear you. I just don't want to open my eyes. Don't be fearful."

When John did try to pray, his words were hesitant as though to ask God to heal me might bring him a disappointment. I caught the same cautious tone from preachers as well as lay people. They were praying, "We ask that Your will be done with this desperately sick woman." I understand the reluctance some people have to pray with all-out faith. From the viewpoint of having been a very sick woman, hedged prayers almost made me feel that God was a capricious Father who couldn't be trusted to do the right thing by His children.

My mother had to care for our six-year-old during the first days after the operation. When she walked into my hospital room for the first time, she looked at my greenish face, gasped and slumped to the floor. A nurse was summoned while Daddy lifted her into a chair and began rubbing her wrists. She revived quickly but spent the rest of her visit talking in a whisper as though afraid to waken me. I wanted to comfort Mother somehow. "I know I must look awful, Mother, but I'm aware of what is going on. Please don't whisper. I want to hear what you're saying. And don't be so melodramatic. Just tell me about Brenda and Gary."

It was almost as if Mother heard me. The next time she visited my room accompanied by her older sister, my Aunt Lillian, she was much more positive. While making a tour of the flowers that had been sent by relatives and friends, she directed her conversation to me.

"Betty, you may not hear me," Mother said, "but I think I'll read you these get-well cards and describe the flower arrangements." She did so with help from her sister.

Then Aunt Lillian, who was the principal of the Marion Heights Elementary School in northwest Terre Haute, spoke of a visit she had had with Brenda.

"Brenda can't understand why she isn't allowed to visit you, Bets. She says she doesn't have any germs that would hurt you. Meanwhile, she's been visiting her daddy at work and asked for the job of cleaning the windshield of every car that stops for gas. She says she wants to earn money to help pay your hospital bill.

"Gary wants you to know that he was out to the lake Saturday and has learned to float on his back. And he has taught Brenda to ride the two-wheeler bike. Your mother is so good with them, Bets."

On they went, chatting about family news as though I were wide awake and alert. How I loved it! When they got up to leave and stood by my bed, I tried to open my eyes. All they did was flutter. But the two women noticed and got excited.

"I believe Betty does know we're here," Mother said. Each kissed me tenderly. My spirit was so refreshed by their visit.

Aunt Gertrude was another who knew exactly how to

handle herself when she visited me. She would stride into the room, pick up my hand and hold it gently but firmly. "Keep your chin up, Bets. You'll be home with your family soon. And just remember this, too—we need you back playing the organ at our church."

Each time the words were different, but there was always a life line thrown to me with a ringing affirmation that I would soon get back into the action. And I began to believe I would.

One day I heard the footsteps of a man entering my room and at first assumed they belonged to either my husband or my father. The steps stopped at the foot of my bed. I heard the pages of a book being turned. When he started to read, I recognized the voice of Art Lindsey—the man who had annoyed me so much with his radio program of sermonettes and country music:

> Oh give thanks to the Lord,
> for he is good;
> for his steadfast love endures
> forever!

At first I was so conscious of the man I didn't hear the words. "Why is he here?" I asked myself. "Doesn't he know how sick I am? Only close relatives should come in here."

> Some wandered in desert wastes,
> Finding no way to a city to
> dwell in;
> hungry and thirsty,
> their soul fainteth within them.
> Then they cried to the Lord in
> their trouble,

and he delivered them from
their distress. . . .

As Art read on I calmed down and listened to the words:

> Some were sick through their
> sinful ways,
> And because of their iniquities
> suffered affliction;
> They loathed any kind of food,
> and they drew near to the gates
> of death.
> Then they cried to the Lord in
> their trouble,
> And he delivered them from
> their distress;
> He sent forth his word, and
> healed them,
> And delivered them from destruction.
> Let them thank the Lord for his
> steadfast love,
> For his wonderful works to the
> sons of men!
> And let them offer sacrifices of
> thanksgiving,
> And tell of his deeds in songs
> of joy!
>
> (Psalm 107: 1, 4–6, 17–22)

The words ended like a benediction, filling my soul with hope. How gentle and loving and dedicated was this man! As he walked from the room, I knew that Art Lindsey was indeed God's messenger of good news. I knew too that God had used Art to continue His work inside me, teaching me, healing me, changing me. For in a period of minutes I found myself filled with love for a man I had disliked heartily before.

Once again it had been the Word of God which spoke to me so clearly. This phrase leaped out: *He sent forth his word and healed them.* Was this His way of telling me I would get well? Faith that I would be healed began to turn and whirl like a small wheel within my innermost being.

5

SPIRIT TO SPIRIT

SOON AFTER THE second operation to repair the bowel situation, the infection inside me went wild. My temperature soared to 105 degrees again. When the nurses began having trouble irrigating the stomach pump inside me, the doctor discovered an abscess under the first incision. Back to surgery again for minor repair, with more blood transfusions and the continuous intravenous feedings.

One of the nurses who took care of me during that period was Mary Barton. In recent years I have been in touch with Mary, who now lives in Tucson, Arizona. She vividly recalls some of the desperate moments we shared. There was the growing problem of finding veins strong enough to take the blood transfusions and intravenous feeding. They used the wrists, the bends in both arms, the ankles, and once my big toe, a most painful solution.

During my first days in the hospital I was only aware of events going on about me at a subconscious level. Gradually I began to take a more active interest in the routines.

I kept asking the nurses for pieces of ice to suck. When I once asked Mary Barton if I would ever enjoy food again, she replied, "Yes. And when you do, what would you most like to eat?"

I thought a moment. "A chocolate ice cream soda."

"When the time comes, I'll see that you get it myself," she replied.

She admitted to me later that she was sure this was one promise she would not have to keep.

Another problem the doctors had in battling my infection was in finding enough blood for transfusions. There was a scarcity of my type—B-negative. Radio announcements were repeatedly made for donors but the response was poor. After my second surgery there was a tense, desperate period when the hospital sought frantically for B-negative blood to give me a transfusion. When my father heard of this need, he stood at the foot of my bed to "pray in" the person with this blood type to serve as a donor for me.

The way the Lord answers prayer is fascinating. My uncle, Jesse Scott Mullins, was a brakeman for the Pennsylvania Railroad at the time, the vibrant jolly man who used to toss me about like a sack of potatoes at picnics when I was a girl. He traveled the freights on a run that went from Terre Haute to Peoria to St. Louis and back, riding the caboose, a job that made him the most glamorous man in my life. Once he took me for a short ride in the caboose, pure enchantment for this small girl. On other occasions he would bring us some fusees, the torches railroaders would light on the tracks to warn approaching trains of an obstruction or stalled train. We would light the fusees in our backyard and have picnics by this glamorous reddish-yellow glow.

At the time of my second operation, Uncle Jesse was on his way from Peoria to Terre Haute. Later he told me the full story of what happened:

As Jesse "dead-headed" into Terre Haute, he had a sudden inner feeling that he should stop at the hospital on his way home to give a pint of blood for me. My uncle was not aware of any crisis situation at Union Hospital for B-negative blood. He didn't even know what type of blood he had. All he wanted to do was help John and me keep our hospital bills down.

It was late morning and Jesse was tired and grimy from long hours on the train. It made more sense, he told himself, to go home and shower and rest first, then go to the hospital at night during visiting hours. So he climbed into his car and headed for home. Uncle Jesse had always believed that the supernatural power of God can direct our everyday lives. Therefore, when for the second time he felt an inner nudge to head for Union Hospital, he didn't just slough it off. The feeling would not go away, so despite all his logic and common-sense reasoning, he found himself going directly to the hospital from the roundhouse.

Upon arriving at the hospital, Jesse inquired about the blood donor program and asked if his gift of blood could be credited to a patient who needed transfusions. They said this could be worked out and then drew blood to get his type. Soon a nurse rushed back in a state of urgency and said that Jesse had B-negative blood which at that moment was desperately needed for me. The timing was amazing. It was God alone who did it.

The infusion of Uncle Jesse's blood helped me rally. Later he came by to tease me: "I was your uncle by marriage before. Now I'm your blood uncle."

After surviving this crisis, I began straining to be a mother and wife again. "How is Brenda doing?" I asked my parents. The reassurances that my daughter was fine didn't quite satisfy me. Mother then patiently described in detail the cookies she and Brenda had made, the four new puppies that Dusty, their family dog, had delivered and how Brenda was helping Dusty keep track of her new offspring.

Several times Brenda and Gary had been put on the phone to talk to me. I heard from Gary how Brenda had hogged the one fishing pole when they went to the lake and from Brenda how she had helped Daddy and Papaw teach Gary to water-ski.

Since hospital rules forbade children under fourteen from visiting patients, the next evening they took her to the hospital lawn. "You and Mamaw sit here on the grass by those petunias," my father said, "and when I get to your Mommie's room I'll wave out the window to you. She's on the third floor. Count over four windows from the end and watch for me."

"Will Mama wave out the window, too?" Brenda wanted to know.

"Not today, but soon," Dad replied.

When he announced that Brenda was outside, I could barely nod my head. "Will someone be sure that Brenda gets to see the fireworks on the Fourth of July?" I asked.

Gently my father told me that it was now the sixth of July and that Brenda had already gotten to see the fireworks. Somehow I had lost several days.

In some ways I was more troubled about John than Brenda. My husband followed a certain ritual when he visited me. He would come into my room, kiss me lightly on the forehead or cheek, pat my arm, and then restlessly walk about or assume his sitting position on the other side of the door.

One day when he came into the room I held on to his hand. "Please stay close to me, John," I whispered. Then, summoning up all my strength, I reminded him of the miracle of Brenda.

John and I sat there reminiscing, our minds going back seven years. We had already been married four years without children. The doctor's report had been discouraging. Because of the rheumatic fever John had suffered at age nine and a later hernia condition, John's sperm count had reached an almost zero fertility rate.

We had not given in to this verdict. Once when the pastor in our church asked people to come forward for special prayer, John was the first in line. He had never told me until later that this was a request that he become a father.

While John was praying in church, I would talk to God about the situation every day in my bedroom. One morning I was reading the book of Isaiah. Suddenly these words sprang from the pages:

> For I will pour water upon him that is thirsty,
> and floods upon the dry ground:
> I will pour my spirit upon thy seed,
> and my blessing upon thine offspring.
> (Isaiah 44:3, KJV)

What a blessed promise! To think that the Lord would pour His Spirit and blessing on John and me. It was an awesome moment. I knew then that He was beginning to prepare me for motherhood.

Six weeks later I broke the news to John that I was

pregnant. He wept as he told me for the first time how hard he had prayed for this to happen.

Then came a crisis during the fourth month after a long automobile trip to spend Thanksgiving dinner with John's grandparents. The next morning I began hemorrhaging and called the doctor who came and examined me. He put me to bed but warned that it was probably too late to save the baby. I did not give up. Before going to bed John and I prayed for the Lord to save our child. I rarely dream but that night I saw Jesus coming toward me, holding a tiny baby in His arms.

I started to cry, thinking that I had miscarried and that Jesus had taken the child with Him to heaven. But I was wrong: Jesus walked slowly toward me and laid the child in my arms. I awoke the next morning arms folded across my stomach, still holding the baby inside my body.

Six months later on Father's Day, June 21, 1953, Brenda was born, a healthy and normal baby in every way.

Remembering how God had spared our unborn child strengthened John. From then on he stayed inside the room and was much more relaxed. One day he came in after spending the day with Brenda. I was asleep when he arrived, but soon awoke as John began relating his experiences to my Dad.

"Brenda and I really had fun today," he said. "I took her home so she could play for a while with her old friends, with her toys and in her sand pile. Then I took her to the station. She wanted to wash some car windows, so I let her do it with customers I knew well. She had a ball.

"On the way home, I told her I would cook supper and asked her what she wanted. She told me 'Sandburgers.'" (This was Brenda's term for a hamburger sandwich.)

At this point I was so interested I opened my eyes and tried to focus on my husband. John had never fixed a meal even once in our marriage, and would have been horrified if asked to put on an apron. He would not know where to find the salt and pepper, much less how to put meat into a skillet and use the stove correctly.

But I could see that John was relaxed and enjoying his role as storyteller. "So, Brenda and I stopped at the store, grabbed a cart, and bought some groceries. When we got home, I spread out the hamburger, tomatoes, lettuce, onion, mustard on the table. Then I got a frying pan, and opened the package of hamburger, formed a nice little 'sandburger' for Brenda and put it in the skillet.

"My first mistake. I had picked up ground pork sausage, instead of hamburger. Oh, well. Smothered with lettuce, tomatoes, onions and mustard, Brenda wouldn't know the difference.

"My second mistake. When I opened the cellophane around the lettuce I saw it was cabbage. Oh, well. Lettuce and cabbage are almost the same thing. So I fried the patty, put the sausage on the cabbage, plus all the other stuff, and served it to Brenda.

"Poor kid. She took one bite, pushed it aside and said, 'Daddy, I like gravy. Will you make me some gravy and put it on bread pieces for me? That'll be okay, Daddy.' I could see that this kid still had faith in me.

"I thought making gravy would be a breeze. . . . Just add some flour to that stuff in the skillet. Well, I must have put in too much flour. It was awful thick. Brenda took one bite and said, 'Hey, Daddy, I got it. Let's go to the Royal Chef.'

"That sounded like a great idea to me. But before we left,

I didn't want to throw away all that good gravy. So I dumped it out in the cat's bowl. Pumpkin Face had been staring at us hungrily ever since we brought her over from the neighbors for the day. Well, Pumpkin Face took one lick, shivered and walked away. The ingratitude of that cat!"

My father was laughing so hard he almost fell out of his chair. It didn't seem quite that funny to me, but it was good to see that John was getting back his sense of humor. And I was reassured over how much my family needed me.

Later that night I found myself dreaming. John was in the kitchen frying "sandburgers" and there was this awful smoke coming from the stove. I was in bed and couldn't move. . . . I tried desperately to get out of bed, but my legs seemed paralyzed. . . . I kept trying to call John to turn off the oven, but I could not open my mouth.

I woke up in a panic. My hospital room was dark; only a dim light filtered through the slightly ajar door. Desperately I reached out for the warm Presence that had comforted me during bad moments in recent days. "Lord, help me. Lord, will I ever get well? Please take away the pain."

At once the throbbing in my head eased slightly. My panic subsided. I was not alone. The Comforter had returned. Then gently, but firmly, I felt Him probing into my life again. "What did you learn today from your husband?" The question was there in my mind and I'm sure I didn't ask it of myself. My husband's pathetic effort to cook a meal showed how much he needed me.

"That's what you want, isn't it, Betty? To have your family totally dependent on you?"

Again, this thought had come from the outside. It was a bit disconcerting; but not nearly as disturbing as the next thought.

"When John and Brenda are so dependent on you, Betty, they do not need Me."

By now I was wide awake. This thought deeply disturbed me. Was I blocking my husband and daughter from God?

I fought off a desire to turn away from these painful revelations about myself, but there was no condemnation in the Presence. Only loving concern. Then it seemed that the two of us were seated side by side in front of a screen on which a series of scenes from my life were flashed.

Scene: My parents, younger brothers and I are driving in our old Hudson car to church on a hot summer day. The car has no air conditioning, yet I angrily shout at my sweltering brothers that the windows must be kept shut or my hairdo will be ruined.

Scene: Our kitchen soon after my marriage to John. At 5:30 A.M. I am baking biscuits when John sleepily appears, asking why the early rising. "I want your mother to know that you have a wife who gets up early every morning to fix your breakfast."

Scene: In a local department store I spend hours trying to find matching mother-daughter outfits for Brenda and me. I explain the intensity of my search to the clerk: "It gives my daughter a sense of security to dress like her mommy."

Scene: Late at night in our bedroom. I give the room a romantic aura by lighting some candles. Next comes a spray of perfume. John watches me from the bed with mixed emotions. "Just one time I'd like you to forget the trappings, come into my arms and say that all you really want is me," he says.

Scene: John and I are talking one evening in our home. He has met a young husband and wife who have had such

71

marital troubles that their infidelities are well known about town. "They're looking for help," says John, "and I'd like to have them for dinner and then take them to our church afterwards." I tell John that the neighbors might think it strange if we identify with people of low reputation, that it would be best for them to go to church directly and have my father minister to their needs.

All of these scenes on the surface might seem fairly typical of family life. Yet as each one flashed before me I was gently made aware of a truth about myself.

My determination to protect my hairdo in the car, at the expense of others, was not only self-centeredness, it was the beginning of a pattern to get my own way.

My early arising to bake biscuits was not to show John how much I loved him, but to impress others with what a good wife I was.

My great search to find matching mother-daughter outfits was not for Brenda's security as much as an effort to tie my daughter closer to me.

The candles and perfume act was not to make it easier for me to give myself more completely to my husband. It was a bit of fantasy on my part to make our physical relationship seem better than it was and to give me story material to impress others with the romantic quality of our marriage.

My turndown of the adulterous couple was the most devastating scene of all. Seeing my self-righteousness and pride made me want to hide my head under the pillow in shame. How this act must have grieved the Spirit of God. Tears flowed down my cheeks. "Forgive me, Lord. Forgive me."

The Presence did not have to say a word, nor did He

try to soften the impact. I felt awed by the exposure of my selfish, arrogant nature. When the tears of repentance came, there was comfort and reassurance in His manner. And then once again I saw on the screen His Word for me in clear block letters: *Thou shalt have no other gods before me*.

The image faded; the Presence was gone. I raised myself from my pillow slightly to look about my hospital room. The hum of the window air-conditioner was unchanged. The bottle of liquid nourishment suspended behind my head continued to drip-drip through the tubing into my veins. The drain from my abdominal cavity continued to draw off poison into a jar underneath the bed. Everything was unchanged outside of myself. Inside I was different. I reached the call button to ask the nurse for another small piece of ice for my parched lips.

6

THE CRISIS POINT

THE DAYS WENT BY; the month of July was almost over. Six weeks had passed since the first attack of appendicitis. Yet I was still fighting for my life as doctors tried different drugs to clean out the poison in my system. By now I had gone through four rounds of surgery, and my weight was down to eighty pounds. John and my parents were near exhaustion from the daily bedside rituals.

I learned later that the final crisis was brought on by pneumonia. What little resistance I had left was sharply eroded by this new invasion of germs. Nurse Mary Barton had the shift from 3:00 to 11:00 P.M. and was monitoring my vital signs carefully. Both Dad and Mother were in the room the afternoon of the emergency.

It happened around 4:30 P.M. Mary had come in to check the I-V equipment because several times when the needle had been inserted, a collapsed vein had rejected the fluids. Little bubbles had formed in several places on my skin where this had happened.

Suddenly she grabbed my hand and took my pulse. There was none. Startled, she looked at the pupils of my eyes. Then she called for emergency equipment. All my parents could do was watch helplessly and pray.

There followed a tense desperate drama as both the doctor on duty and several nurses used emergency measures to get my heart, pulse and blood pressure functioning again. By the time my vital signs were back to normal Dr. Bherne and John had arrived. The strain was too much for Mother. She fainted and a nurse ministered to her. The doctor then pulled my father aside and told him that he felt it would be only a matter of hours before I slipped away. He said quite frankly that death might be the best solution. He suspected that I might have such severe brain damage, plus the extensive assault on other internal organs by gangrene, that I could never live a normal life.

Depressed and exhausted, Dad decided to drive my mother home, get some sleep and return early the next morning. John, who was now spending his nights at my parents' home with Brenda, decided he would close his Sunoco station early and join Mother and Dad and the children for a late supper.

Here again, I learned about the events which followed from my parents, especially Dad. And it was strange how certain experiences in Dad's early life were to affect the present crisis.

During the thirty-one-mile drive back to their home in Clay City, Mother did most of the talking. "I just can't believe God wants to take a vital twenty-seven-year-old woman from her husband and daughter. She's needed here, Glenn. Why, Betty has only begun to live."

"God doesn't take a young wife away from her husband

and child in a cold-blooded manner, Fern," my father answered. "Often we don't understand why things happen the way they do until later, but we know that we must trust Him to do what's best in the long run for His children."

"But God can heal Betty?"

"Yes. He certainly can."

"Then let's keep praying that He will."

In a few minutes, Mother's depression returned. "Where will we bury Betty? Do you think John will let us bury her in our family plot—or will he want a plot of his own?"

Once again my father tried to comfort Mother; both were silent during the rest of the drive home.

As Dad walked into his study, his first thought was to read something from Scripture. Then he noticed on his desk five cards lined up in a row—five Father's Day remembrances received many weeks before from each of his children, four sons and one daughter. Once again he read the words I had written to him:

Dear Daddy,

Happy Papa's Day to thee! . . . from me! You have been more than a Dad. You've been a priest and teacher too. I didn't realize until I became a parent myself, how much like Jesus you are. You are the son of a carpenter, as He was, learning to work with your hands with wood and shavings . . . even building churches both structurally and spiritually.

There are men who sire children, but are not fathers. There are mothers who are merely incubators. You and Mother have nurtured me, introduced me to God. You were my first church, and this child's first university.

Your ugliest daughter,
(the only one too)
Betsy

76

Tears streaming down his face, Dad told me later how he sat there for a long time, praying for the faith to believe that his only daughter could get well. Then he remembered another time years before when he had no faith at all. Glenn Perkins was twenty-two, newly married, and barely making a living back in 1930 as a mechanic in a glass factory. His young wife, Fern, was desperately sick with uremic poisoning. Her fingernails had turned purple. The doctor had packed her in ice to bring down her temperature and felt an operation might give her a fifty-fifty chance to live.

A group of Fern's church friends and the pastor came to pray. They were so noisy about it that Glenn, a nonbeliever, took off for the woods. Hours later he returned to find his wife standing in the middle of the room singing hymns and praising God. She had been healed.

After this example of a miracle-working God, Glenn Perkins began studying the Bible and attending services. One night he was reading the second chapter of Acts.

"Suddenly the black Bible began to glow in my hands," he told us later. "It seemed to be on fire. Then the house began to shake. It was the Upper Room all over again. I shouted at Fern: 'Pray for me, honey. Something's wrong.' I didn't know what to do. I didn't think I could stand it."

At the next church service my father went forward and accepted Jesus Christ as Savior and Lord. When this happened, I was six months old.

Dad then began attending Bible school in his spare time, while making a living as a carpenter. In the fall of 1932 my father was impressed by a visiting preacher named Kenneth Wilkerson, who was starting a new church in nearby Attica, Indiana. Wilkerson's congregation was meeting above a grocery store. Dad was hired as a carpenter by Pastor Wilkerson to help build a new church, using volunteers from the congregation.

It was a severe winter, volunteers were scarce and Kenneth Wilkerson and my father did most of the construction themselves. It was so cold and money was so scarce that Dad often had to round up sacks of dried corncobs from a feed mill to burn in the potbellied stove to keep them warm while they worked. When the church was finished, my father stayed on to assist Kenneth Wilkerson, teaching, leading the singing, counseling young people.

One of Kenneth Wilkerson's sons was a boy named David. He was a mixed-up youth, bored with the church and skeptical of the spiritual convictions of his parents. Then the Holy Spirit touched David Wilkerson and revolutionized his life. Later, when David was led by God to come to New York City to minister to disturbed teenagers, this marked the beginning of Teen Challenge and formed the basis for *The Cross and the Switchblade*, David Wilkerson's international bestselling book.

Although he could barely provide for his family during those depression years of the thirties, my father could not deny the call of God on his life. As he sat at his desk praying for me that bleak summer night in 1959, feeling strong assaults on his faith, Dad remembered another occasion when the Lord used him in a dramatic way.

It happened in the middle of a snowy night in the early thirties. Dad suddenly awoke. One unsuccessful effort to go back to sleep made him realize that the Lord had awakened him and wanted him to do something. Mother was sleeping serenely beside him, and everything in the house seemed to be in order.

Then he was given a message in the form of a clear, strong inner directive. He was told to go down to the business district of west Terre Haute. Someone was there in desperate need. This was a time when Indiana was hard-hit by the depression.

At first, Dad was not sure that he had heard correctly. Would he not feel foolish dressing and going to town in the middle of the night? What if he found nothing but snowy, deserted streets?

Kneeling down by the bed, he asked for verification of what he thought he had heard. Immediately, he felt God's presence and lines from a hymn were dropped into his mind:

Rescue the perishing,
Care for the dying . . .

By then Mother was awake. He explained what had happened, got dressed, bundled up, and started for town.

As he strode along briskly, trying to keep warm, he wondered what he would do if there were several people on the streets. How would he know the person he was being sent to help? He concluded that if God would send him on an errand like this, He could surely be trusted to handle such details.

When Dad got to the main street there was but one person in sight, a man leaning against a lamppost, his head down. With a quick prayer, asking the Lord to protect and guide him, Dad approached the stranger. "Is there any way I can help you?"

The man must have seen kindness and compassion in

79

Dad's face for the story came pouring out. "My wife and I have quarreled because I can't make a living for my family. I've tried and tried, but I can't find a job. I'm useless, worthless. I've been trying to decide whether to lie down in front of the early morning freight or kill myself with this gun in my pocket. But I *am* going to end it all."

He paused for breath, his eyes searching Dad's face. "Sir, I'd like to ask you, what would you do if you were me?"

Promptly came the answer. "Sir, if it were me, I would turn my life over to Almighty God who loves me and who has promised to supply all my needs."

The two men talked earnestly for a while, then knelt down on the snowy sidewalk while the desperate man handed his life over to Jesus. He then went home to his family and began a new life.

Dad told us later, "I've scarcely ever felt such joy as at that moment. It seemed that all of Heaven was shouting hosannas. I know something of Jesus' great joy when in our extremity, any of us allows Him to be our Savior and gives Him the chance to save us from our problems."

My father went into the fulltime ministry soon after that experience and became a loving, patient, sensitive pastor beloved by his flock.

When John arrived, Mother and Dad rounded up Gary and Brenda and at eight o'clock the five had a subdued meal together. The children had questions which no one wanted to answer. What was there to say? Everyone was taut with fatigue and discouragement. John's silence and the haunted look on his face especially troubled Dad, he told me later.

Then Dad asked everyone to hold hands around the table as he prayed: "Lord Jesus, we love You and praise You for the good things of life You have given us. We thank You for Betty, for trusting us with her these years. We relinquish her to You now, knowing how much You love her too. Be with her now, Lord, as she struggles for life. Mend her body, soothe her mind, heal her spirit. Forgive us for our lack of faith and our weaknesses, Lord. We want only to serve You. Amen."

At 3:30 A.M. Dad suddenly awoke. A look at his watch told him it was too early to get up. But when he tried to close his eyes, he felt the same inner prodding he had years before on that snowy night in the middle of the depression. The Lord was asking him to get up and go now to the hospital. Betty needed him!

My father arose, shaved, dressed and had some toast and a cup of coffee. He then awoke John. When he slipped out of the house it was about 4:15 A.M. Dad took Highway 41 from Clay City direct to southern Terre Haute and Union Hospital. The drive took him about forty-five minutes. John left a few minutes later for his station.

Shortly after 5:00 A.M. the telephone awakened my mother. She answered in sudden panic. The woman introduced herself as the night nurse on the third floor of Union Hospital.

"Mrs. Perkins, I'm sorry to call you at this hour, but I have bad news. Your daughter, Betty, passed away a few minutes ago. We can't reach her husband. Will you try and locate him and ask him to come to the hospital as soon as possible to make the necessary arrangements? If Mr. Upchurch can't be reached, will you ask your husband to come to the hospital as soon as possible?"

Mother pulled herself together as best she could. "My

husband is on his way to the hospital right now. Please intercept him before he goes to Betty's room. Seeing his daughter's body will be a great shock to him."

The nurse promised she would be on the lookout for Dad and hung up. Mother lay down on her pillow and sobbed.

In his own words, here is Dad's account of what happened when he arrived at the hospital:

"It was still dark when I parked my car near the back of the hospital. The time: about 5:00 A.M. There were faint streaks of light in the sky as I walked toward the nurses' entrance because it was a much more direct route to Betty's room. I climbed the two flights of stairs and headed for Betty's room, number 336. Down the hall, I saw the black nurse's aide leave Betty's room and close the door. This was unusual; always before the door had been open.

"I knocked softly on Betty's door. There was no answer. I opened the door and walked inside.

"The room seemed very dark and still. And empty. As my eyes adjusted to the gloom, I first noticed the absence of the life-supporting equipment. Startled, my eyes swung to the bed.

"A sheet had been pulled up over Betty's head!

"Slowly the facts worked to a conclusion in my mind: Betty was dead. I stood there for several minutes in frozen silence as feelings of grief flooded my emotions. Then all that I felt focused on one word which I spoke several times fervently.

"Jesus . . . Jesus . . . Jesus.

"It was a plea, a moan and a prayer. It was also the only word that ever made sense to me in times of great bewilderment, or pain or sorrow. I don't know how long I stood there beside the bed. I only remember that the room lightened as the sun began to slip through the curtains.

"Then my eyes were caught by something. Did I see a slight movement in the sheet covering Betty?"

7

THE CITY OF TOMORROW

MY MEMORY OF the late-afternoon crisis and the rest of
that day is blurred. Dimly I recall a crowded room, slipping into a coma, then coming out of it. I was vaguely
aware that my parents left my hospital room first, John
sometime later, that Nurse Barton watched me closely before she went off duty, that a young nurse's aide was in and
out of my room during the night.

It must have been sometime around 5:00 A.M. when my
body functions apparently stopped, much as they had earlier
in the day. Only this time there was no one at my bedside
to call for the emergency equipment.

The transition was serene and peaceful. I was walking up
a beautiful green hill. It was steep, but my leg motion was
effortless and a deep ecstasy flooded my body. Despite three
incisions in my body from the operations, I stood erect without pain, enjoying my tallness, free from inhibitions about
it. I looked down. I seemed to be barefoot, but the complete
outer shape of my body was a blur and colorless. Yet I was
walking on grass, the most vivid shade of green I had ever

seen. Each blade was perhaps one inch long, the texture like fine velvet; every blade was vibrant and moving. As the bottoms of my feet touched the grass, something alive in the grass was transmitted up through my whole body with each step I took.

"Can this be death?" I wondered. If so, I certainly had nothing to fear. There was no darkness, no uncertainty, only a change in location and a total sense of well-being.

All around me was a magnificent deep blue sky, unobscured by clouds. Looking about, I realized that there was no road or path. Yet I seemed to know where to go.

Then I realized I was not walking alone. To the left, and a little behind me, strode a tall, masculine-looking figure in a robe. I wondered if he were an angel and tried to see if he had wings. But he was facing me and I could not see his back. I sensed, however, that he could go anywhere he wanted and very quickly.

We did not speak to each other. Somehow it didn't seem necessary, for we were both going in the same direction. Then I became aware that he was not a stranger. He knew me and I felt a strange kinship with him. Where had we met? Had we always known each other? It seemed we had. Where were we now going?

As we walked together I saw no sun—but light was everywhere. Off to the left there were multicolored flowers blooming. Also trees, shrubs. On the right was a low stone wall.

Once years before I had climbed to the top of Logan's Pass in Glacier National Park, breathing the pure, clean, unused air amidst the snowcapped peaks. There were small flowers blooming even in the snow. My legs had been sore and tired from that climb.

This climb was different. My legs were not tired and I

wasn't aware of any temperature. There was no snow, though I seemed to be in a high altitude. There seemed to be no seasons but it felt like early spring. My emotion was a combination of feelings: youth, serenity, fulfillment, health, awareness, tranquillity. I felt I had everything I ever wanted to have. I was everything I had ever intended to be. I was arriving at where I had always dreamed of being.

The wall to my right was higher now and made of many-colored, multi-tiered stones. A light from the other side of the wall shone through a long row of amber-colored gems several feet above my head. "Topaz," I thought to myself. "The November birthstone." I remembered this from working in Edwards Jewelry store in New Castle, Indiana, before my marriage to John. November 6th is my birthday.*

Just as we crested the top of the hill, I heard my father's voice calling, "Jesus, Jesus, Jesus." His voice was a long distance away. I thought about turning back to find him. I did not because I knew my destination was ahead. We walked along in silence save for the whisper of a gentle breeze ruffling the white, sheer garments of the angel.

We came upon a magnificent, silver structure. It was like a palace except there were no towers. As we walked toward it, I heard voices. They were melodious, harmonious, blending in chorus and I heard the word, "Jesus." There were more than four parts to their harmony. I not only heard the singing and felt the singing but I joined the singing. I have always had a girl's body, but a low boy's voice. Sud-

---

* Editor's note: Betty was later to discover that the 21st chapter of Revelation, verses 19–20, described the heavenly city whose walls were to be adorned with precious stones. The first foundation was jasper; the second sapphire . . . the ninth, topaz. If each foundation was about a foot high, this would place topaz about three feet higher than Betty's head.

denly I realized I was singing the way I had always wanted to . . . in high, clear and sweet tones.

After a while the music softened, then the unseen voices picked up a new chorus. The voices not only burst forth in more than four parts, but they were in different languages. I was awed by the richness and perfect blending of the words—and I could understand them! I do not know why this was possible except that I was part of a universal experience.

While the angel and I walked together I sensed we could go wherever we willed ourselves to go and be there instantly. Communication between us was through the projection of thoughts. The words sung in all the different languages were understandable, but I don't know how or why. We all seemed to be on some universal wave length.

I thought at the time, "I will never forget the melody and these words." But later I could only recall two: "Jesus" and "redeemed."

The angel stepped forward and put the palm of his hand upon a gate which I had not noticed before. About twelve feet high, the gate was a solid sheet of pearl, with no handles and some lovely scroll work at the top of its Gothic structure. The pearl was translucent so that I could almost, but not quite, see inside. The atmosphere inside was somehow filtered through. My feeling was of ecstatic joy and anticipation at the thought of going inside.

When the angel stepped forward, pressing his palm on the gate, an opening appeared in the center of the pearl panel and slowly widened and deepened as though the translucent material was dissolving. Inside I saw what appeared to be a street of golden color with an overlay of glass or water. The yellow light that appeared was dazzling.

There is no way to describe it. I saw no figure, yet I was conscious of a Person. Suddenly I knew that the light was Jesus, the Person was Jesus.

I did not have to move. The light was all about me. There seemed to be some heat in it as if I were standing in sunlight; my body began to glow. Every part of me was absorbing the light. I felt bathed by the rays of a powerful, penetrating, loving energy.

The angel looked at me and communicated the thought: "Would you like to go in and join them?"

I longed with all my being to go inside, yet I hesitated. Did I have a choice? Then I remembered my father's voice. Perhaps I should go and find him.

"I would like to stay and sing a little longer, then go back down the hill!" I finally answered. I started to say something more. But it was too late.

The gates slowly melted into one sheet of pearl again and we began walking back down the same beautiful hill. This time the jeweled wall was on my left and the angel walked on my right.

Then I saw the sun coming up over the wall. This surprised me since it was already very light and there seemed to be no passing of time. It was a lovely sunrise. The topaz and other stones glowed brilliantly. I remember noticing that the wall now made a deep shadow on my side.

Walking down the hill I looked into Terre Haute as the worlds of spirit and time and space began to fuse back together. Ahead of me were many church steeples glistening in the morning sun. I was suddenly aware of God's love for all His churches. It was a sudden bit of knowledge, as if I were being told this on the inside by the Holy Spirit. At that moment I loved all His churches too; and as my prejudices dissolved, I loved all His people.

Then I saw the tops of trees, then the hospital. My eyes seemed to bore through the walls of the hospital like laser beams, down the hall of the third floor to Room 336. I saw a figure on the bed with a sheet pulled over it.

After my descent I slowed down and stopped. The sun's rays were in my eyes. There were dust particles in the light which suddenly changed to wavy letters about two inches high flashing before me like a ticker-tape message. The letters seemed composed of translucent ivory, only fluid—moving through the rays of sun.

I was back in my hospital bed now and the letters stretched all the way from the window, past my bed and on into the room. They read: *I am the resurrection and the life; he that believeth in me, though he were dead, yet shall he live.*

The words were so alive that they pulsated. I knew that I had to touch those living words. I reached up and out and pushed the sheet off my face. At that instant the Word of God literally became life to me. The warmth in the moving letters flowed into my fingers and up my arm. I sat up in bed!

No man can claim credit for my healing. *The Lord had sent forth His WORD and healed me* (Ps. 107:20). Days before, the man Art had read this Scripture at the foot of my bed.

Promise became reality . . . hope became fact.

My father was staring at me in a state of shock. I noticed him only for a moment. I was still seeking out the unearthly light in the room, determined to find its source. My eyes went to the window. Outside was a glorious sight —the green grass on the lawn of the hospital. I had been too sick to see it before, too busy for years to notice how beautiful green grass can be.

Then I saw another beautiful sight outside. A black man. He was carrying on his shoulder a case of soft drinks into the building. I had never before cared for black people. Yet I now felt a great love for that man. God was continuing His healing work in me.

At last I looked at my father standing by my bed. He was still stunned, too startled to cry out, or hug me, or shed tears of joy. Rather he was rooted to the spot, struck dumb with awe before the majesty of the working of God.

8

MY CHANGED WORLD

I TRIED TO TELL Dad about the experience I had just been through on the other side, but I don't think he really heard me. He just kept smiling at me and squeezing my hand, tears sliding down his cheeks. His eyes seemed to devour me.

When the young nurse's aide popped into the room and saw me sitting up in bed, she screamed, "Ma'am, you're a ghost!" Her black face was ashen. I reached for her hand, surprised by the warm feeling inside that made me want to hug her and reassure her. "Tell the floor nurse, I'm not only alive, but I feel wonderful."

The young aide scurried away and soon the chief nurse, with a shocked expression on her face, was wheeling back into the room the life support equipment that had been removed. Jubilant calls were made to John, who had just arrived at the station, and Mother.

The nurses wanted to put the tubes back in me but I shook my head. "I'm sure I don't need them any more. I'm hungry. Please tell Dr. Bherne that I want some real food."

Then I picked up the telephone and dialed my elderly paternal grandmother, Mom Perky. She was in her eighties, a gentle, old-fashioned servant of the Lord. "Hello, Mom Perky, this is Betty! Do you believe in miracles? I'm sitting up here in bed feeling great." God love her, she was so confused. She had been ill for a long time and Mother had called just a short time before to tell her I had died. She now thought we were both in heaven and talking there on the phone.

Minutes later John arrived in my room, so moved he didn't quite know what to do. He stood next to Dad, staring at me, trying to understand the journey I had taken. Every now and then he would reach over and pat me on the shoulder, or on my knee or the arm, or my side to see if I was real.

There sure wasn't much left of me—just an emaciated yellowish-green face and a skinny disintegrated eighty-pound skeleton of a body. But how alive I felt!

Dr. Bherne was the next to arrive. I'll probably never know what conversation took place between him and the floor nurse before he walked into my room. He gave me a long, careful look, paying little attention to my excited chatter. Then he began a careful examination. I noticed a tremor in his hand when he applied the stethoscope. Finally, he flashed me a cautious smile.

"You are indeed much better," he said.

"The Lord has healed me," I replied. "I died about an hour ago. I met Him over there and He let me return. It was an incredibly beautiful experience."

The doctor looked uncomfortable. "Some things happen

which we can't explain. Whatever it was—you seem to be much improved."

"How do you explain my sudden recovery?"

He smiled, "I believe in things I can personally explain."

Several of my relatives arrived and the doctor started to leave. "Before you go, Dr. Bherne, I want you to know that I'm very hungry. When do I eat real food?"

It was the first time I had wanted solid food since the night of the bad pain down in Florida.

The doctor shook his head. "You must go very slow on that. Perhaps some 7-Up on ice to start."

The festive air continued in my room all morning as a stream of relatives arrived. It was a victory party. Two more doctors appeared to examine and question me. But the 7-Up on ice never appeared.

Around noon the young nurse's aide brought me a tray. On it were two pork chops, applesauce, cottage cheese, a square of lemon cake with warm sauce and a pot of tea. Hungrily I ate every morsel, thinking it the most delicious food I ever tasted.

Shortly thereafter a flustered nurse came in to examine my tray, pursued by an irate patient named Mrs. Underwood who had been served nothing but a few ounces of 7-Up for lunch. Upchurch and Underwood—it was easy to see how the mix-up occurred. Sure enough, behind the teapot on my tray was a card with Underwood on it.

Minutes later the nurse returned with a mobile unit. "I'm sorry. I'm going to have to pump out your stomach."

Every fiber of my body protested that this was not necessary. "Please . . . please," I insisted. "The food was so good. It went down so smoothly and I feel just fine."

The nurse continued unrolling the tubing. "Orders are orders," she replied.

"I'm sorry," I said more firmly. "But I have lost so much weight that this nourishment is desperately needed." She wavered. "I promise to ring you the moment I think I'm in trouble," I continued.

Reluctantly, the nurse retreated with her unit. "Lord," I prayed, "please help digest this food."

The process of eating, digestion and elimination is so routine with most of us that we never appreciate what a miraculously smooth operation it is until something goes wrong. The next few hours was a time of great suspense. I hadn't eaten real food in weeks. Would the pork and apple-sauce and cottage cheese pass through the digestive tract? If there was a problem, my stomach would quickly flash the warning signal.

Several hours went by as relatives continued to come and go. The body gave its sign and I pushed the call button. When the nurse appeared apprehensively, I flashed her my brightest smile. "Would you help me to the bathroom, please?"

Wobbly as I was, it was like a triumphant procession. And how can I describe my jubilation to find that all my plumbing worked?

The next morning Dr. Bherne closed the door to my room, examined me carefully and then sat down in a chair by the bed. Seeing that he had also adjusted a second chair near his, I pointed to it. "Anyone else coming to this pity party? Or is it a welcome back party?"

He laughed for the first time. "That chair there is for gangrene to set in!" he replied humorously.

I laughed too. How good it sounded!

I liked Dr. Bherne. He had been very negative about my chances; he was a somber man, but a fine doctor, a skilled surgeon. I felt a sudden burst of gratitude for the hours of care he had given me.

Now I really saw him for the first time; a short man with rimless eyeglasses, furrowed brow, graying thinning hair closely cropped. His eyes were friendly, but somewhat disapproving. I sensed he was about to give a sober serious talk about what the illness had done to me.

"I think we can release you from the hospital in a few days," he began. "This is good news, of course. We are delighted by your comeback. But you have been a desperately sick woman for a long time. It will be many months before we know the extent of the damage to your system." Then he went on to tick off the areas which were of concern to him. It seemed that the infection had collided with nearly every organ in my body.

"We did not remove your reproductive organs," he continued, "but I could tell that they were severely damaged by the gangrenous infection. There is such a thin membrane between the appendix and the ovaries that peritonitis is always a severe threat to a woman's fertility. In your case, there is hardly one chance in a hundred that you could conceive, one in a thousand that the baby would be normal. In fact, the odds are probably even worse than that.

"I strongly urge you and your husband to use contraceptives from now on. Considering the massive infection which bombarded your ovaries, I also suggest that you consider having them removed sometime soon. A deformed child is quite a price to pay for carelessness, although I do not believe there is much chance you could conceive under any circumstances."

When he had finished his lecture, the doctor gave me that approving smile he reserved for cooperative patients and left to make his rounds.

It was several days before Nurse Mary Barton returned to duty. She came into the room, stood at the foot of my bed and stared at me, speechless and wide-eyed while I described the healing I had received.

"I just can't believe it," she said. "You were dying when I last saw you." She picked up my chart and stared at it in disbelief. "And you're now back on solid food, too."

All I could do was grin at the bewilderment on her kind face.

Later that afternoon, on her coffee break, Mary crossed the street, entered the fountain of the Walgreen Drug Store and purchased a large chocolate ice cream soda. With a giant-sized smile on her face, Mary Barton then appeared in my room and presented it to me with a great flourish, making good on her promise. "This is one bet I never thought I'd have to pay off," she said.

What a treat it was! I don't know who enjoyed it the most: Mary, the grinning gift-bearer, or Betty, the eager recipient.

Several days later John brought me home. It took two trips to carry the accumulation of flowers, plants, gifts, and personal items. I was still so frail and weak that I could only take a few steps at a time. But what a thrill for John and me to be back in our own home, to lie again together in our bed, to sit across the breakfast table, to hold hands on the living room couch as we watched television, to see Brenda dashing about the house with her dolls and toys, telling friends excitedly, "Mommy's home! Mommy's home!"

What a difference I felt now about my home. Gone was the restlessness, the desire to escape to Florida. Instead, there was a steady continuous feeling of praise. In the hospital the Lord had first helped me see myself and my sinful nature and then through His Word He had shown me what correction was needed. How wonderful to have this personal relationship with Him. How incredible to encounter Jesus personally in His world and to stand in His light and feel the marvelous flow of His health pass through my body!

I began each day with Him, absorbing more of His Word, seeking His Presence with a joyful sound on my lips. One morning as I was to start a recuperative program, there came a clear message on the mirror of my mind: *You shall be like a tree planted by the water.*

Quickly I reached for my Bible and turned to the First Psalm, which is a tribute to the righteous man. There it was—third verse:

And he shall be like a tree planted by the rivers of water,
that bringeth forth his fruit in his season;
his leaf also shall not wither;
and whatsoever he doeth shall prosper.

(KJV)

The more I meditated on this, the more I felt that the Lord would have me key on the word "water," that He was advising me to drink six to eight glasses a day to continue the flushing out of impurities in my system. My skin, my tissue, all my organs were crying for moisture. It is a procedure I have followed to this day, resulting in a long period of good health, no colds, clear skin. Thank you, Lord! (A man who heard me tell about this in a speech, wrote me recently that he had been unable to wear contact lenses until he began drinking six to eight glasses of water per day. Results: more moisture in his eyes and the irritation gone.)

During the months that followed, I slowly built up my body, regained lost weight and watched carefully for problems that Dr. Bherne indicated I might have. There were no aftereffects to the pain-killing drugs. My body functions were normal. My eyesight seemed unimpaired.

Some years later I went to the Bureau of Motor Vehicles to renew my driver's license. I read the charts quickly and easily. The testing officer then asked me to remove my contact lenses and read the fine print on the lower line again. He could not understand the jubilation of my reply when I said, "I'll reread the lower line, but I don't wear contact lenses."

Before my illness I had a fear of high places. Looking down from a tall building made me weak, paralyzed, yet there had been no feelings of fear when I descended from God's City. Nor have I felt any apprehension of high places ever since.

John and I talked and prayed about the possibility of a malformed pregnancy resulting unless we used contraceptives. My inner guidance was that when the Lord heals, He does it completely. John was inclined to follow the doctor's advice—at least for a while. I decided to obey my husband.

The healing was not limited to my body. In addition to dealing with my restless spirit, the Lord cleansed me of lifelong prejudices toward minority groups and a distaste for certain personality types. One of the first persons I sought out was Art Lindsey to thank him personally for the therapy of his visit to me in the hospital. Next was to be Mother Upchurch.

My recuperation period was marred only by John's setback. He came home early from work one day complaining of severe fatigue and went to bed. It was so unlike John I wanted to call the doctor. John said no; he just needed a day or so of rest. Unfortunately this was the time Mother Upchurch chose to visit us.

I had been looking forward to her visit, believing my resentment was gone, determined to have a good relationship with my mother-in-law. When the bell rang late the next morning, I opened the door and embraced her warmly. She was cautiously friendly; her brown eyes studied me for a moment, then swept over the room. She missed nothing; new toys for Brenda, a scatter rug from my parents' home, my new pair of blue shoes.

The moment she entered the living room all her attention was focused on John, who was sitting in a chair in his bathrobe working on the plans for our new house. Her eyes probed every detail of his appearance. Then she launched forth, "John, I'm really worried about you. You look so pale. What's wrong? Why are you home in the middle of the day?"

As always John ignored her solicitations about his health. "I want you to see the plans for our new house," he said.

Mother looked them over, then pursed her lips. "I don't see how you can afford it." Then staring at me, "You two will forever be living beyond your means."

The visit was a disaster. Through it I learned that the healing of my emotions had obviously not gone as deep as I thought.

9

THE SETBACK

MOTHER UPCHURCH's visit was a sharp reverse for me. I thought I was free of my resentment toward her. Now it was back. What bothered me most was that I sensed she was probably right about the new house and John's health, just as she had been right about my spending too much money on things, about holding me responsible for our being in debt so much of the time, and about my being evasive toward her.

But the situation was different now. I cared less about things, more about being a good wife and mother. It was John who was taking the initiative about the new house. I had tried to get John to a doctor but he refused to go. Thus I felt that her accusations toward me were unfair.

While brooding about the situation one morning, it occurred to me that there were several Scriptures that John's mother needed to read. That was the answer. The Word would convict her of her critical nature. Perhaps I should put them in a letter. I reached for a sheet of stationery, then paused. No, the direct approach was better with my mother-in-law. She always said she liked to "call a spade a spade."

I marked the passages and placed the Bible by the telephone. A casual call making reference to the Scriptures would be the way to handle it. The first verse was in Proverbs. With my right hand ready to dial the number, my left turned the pages of the Bible to the chapter.

My eyes fell on the verse. Wait a minute! That wasn't it. Where did that verse come from? I had read through the Bible from beginning to end twice and never recalled that particular verse:

Set a watch, O Lord, before my mouth; keep the door of my lips (Ps. 141:3, KJV).

It was so obvious, I had to laugh. "Lord, You're doing it to me again." I had intended to point the Word against my mother-in-law; instead the Lord turned it around so that it was pointing at me. What a sense of humor He has!

Then I realized that a telephone call wasn't the answer at all; what I really had to do was ask my mother-in-law to forgive me for years of unfriendly words, thoughts and actions against her.

We had been saving for ten years to build our dream house, the plans having been drawn up before my sickness. While John was now eager to go ahead, something inside me was resisting. I should have listened to this Inner Voice but did not and we commissioned the builder to go ahead.

Our new eight-room ranch-style house was built primarily with gray Bedford stone—long, heavy expensive slabs from an Indiana quarry. The design centered around a lavender wrought-iron grape-leaf pattern; we worked it into the trim, shutters, window boxes, porch furniture and on all columns and porch posts. The wallpaper included lavender in the wisteria and lilacs in bloom. Our wall-to-wall carpet was a deep purple; the furniture mostly white. The foundation planting included lilac bushes and wisteria trees.

John regained his vitality following his brief illness, but I noticed his work days were shorter now. He closely supervised the building of our dream house, but did less of the actual work than was in his original plan. When finished, it was beautiful. Yet as we moved in I had no inner joy or elation, and this gave me an uneasy feeling.

One evening the following summer Brenda, now eight, and I were in our new home watching television. The TV picture kept blurring because of thunderstorms in the area. It had been a sultry humid summer day. At sunset the sky was a peculiar yellow-green. I remember wishing that John would close up his business and come home early.

Suddenly at 9:20 P.M. the television picture and sound went haywire as the storm broke overhead. When I turned the set off, a warning system went off inside me and I heard a voice: *You and Brenda get out of this room.*

I started to reason with this warning. "I've never been afraid of storms or the dark or death."

But the voice was insistent. The issue was obedience or not. I grabbed Brenda's hand and we sped from the family room into the bedroom. A moment later there was a sound like a hundred freight cars rumbling and shaking overhead. Looking up, I saw the entire roof separate and blow away from the house. The suction pasted us fast against the wall, bruising my hip. Then I flung Brenda down to the floor and threw my body across her.

The family room we had just left was gone, disintegrated. If I had not obeyed, we both would have been killed.

Brenda and I put our heads under the cherry canopy bed as eight-foot pieces of Bedford stone hurtled about us. The redwood beams broke off and piled up at crazy angles. Then came walls of water in torrents, drenching us, flooding the room so that we had to twist our necks at crazy angles to breathe. A bolt of lightning struck through the debris of our house burning a six-foot circle on the carpet near us.

Brenda was praying out loud. "Oh, Jesus, keep Mommie and me safe. Don't let Smokey (our dog) get hurt. Or Pumpkin Face (our cat). And please, Jesus, don't let my goldfish blow away."

Minutes later, when the wind and the rain stopped, the house was a total ruin. In the garage our new Cadillac car was crushed. The tornado, not even registered at the nearby airport, had destroyed or damaged thirty-six houses in our area.

But Smokey soon wiggled out unhurt from some debris. Pumpkin Face was safe under the crushed car. And to my utter astonishment the glass aquarium was still intact, filled with flecks of debris, to be sure, but all the fish were alive.

When this freakish, capricious tornado struck, I was clad in a sheer white shorty nightgown. As I was helped from the wreckage, a neighbor ran to get me her husband's terrycloth robe which became my chief garment for the next two days. All Brenda had on was a pair of white panties, size four. In twenty seconds, the tornado had demolished possessions which had taken us ten years to accumulate.

When John arrived with the sightseers, repair crews, newspaper reporters and television cameras, we viewed the scene with awe. Plastered against one intact wall was a box of Jello sucked from the kitchen cabinet. The Bible was unruffled on top of the coffee table, one of the few pieces of furniture that remained. The next morning a friend called to say he found our family portraits two and a half miles away in a field. After retrieving them, we returned to our cluttered yard where a reporter from *The Grit* pointed with a smile to an object at the side of our shattered home. There lying in plain view, cover and title up, was a copy of *Gone with the Wind*.

A few individuals pilfered some of our personal belongings, but most people offered help. Our church had a linen shower for us; neighbors loaned us clothing; the insurance company replaced nearly everything, including Brenda's toys; and we were able to rebuild our home within six months.

For days I went around praising Jesus. *The Lord gave, and the Lord has taken away; blessed be the name of the Lord* (Job 1:21). He really is a Savior, I thought to myself. What surprised me more than anything else was my calm at the destruction of prized personal possessions. Things did not matter to me so much since my experience in the hospital. The following verse from a hymn truly described my feelings:

> A tent or a cottage, why should I care?
> They're building a palace for me over there;
> Though exiled from home, yet, still I may sing;
> All glory to God, I'm a child of the King!*

Some months after we had rebuilt our home, John began negotiations to buy a group of gasoline stations throughout the country. I remember the sinking feeling in my stomach

---

* Harriet E. Buell, "A Child of the King."

when he admitted for the first time that the long hours of physical work were too much for him. Operating a chain of stations, he felt, would be less demanding.

When in 1963 John suggested that the time had come to move to Florida, I quickly agreed but for different reasons than I had back in 1959. Florida just might be the place for more relaxed living. So we moved to Clearwater Beach on the west coast of Florida, not too many miles from the Gulf Vista Retreat Center, the scene of my "tummy ache."

John did slow down in Florida, but not through choice. His energy level suddenly dropped again. This time he did go to the hospital for tests. The results were sobering. X-rays of John's heart showed that the aorta valve was shrinking and the heart enlarging. Doctors suggested a valve replacement operation to correct the situation. They warned him it was something he should not postpone. Reluctantly he gave up his idea of setting up a chain of gas stations.

In March of 1963 John and I both went to Gainesville, Florida, so that he could have additional tests at the J. Hillis Miller Heart Center there. We decided to make this a special "get away time" for just the two of us.

We checked into Arrowhead Lodge, which overlooked the campus of the University of Florida Medical School. Our room was on the second floor. I recall thinking that sixteen dollars a day was pretty steep, but that we were not to concern ourselves with economy. As serious as the occasion was, we were to be "joyful unto the Lord."

To this day I remember the room with its blue motif, the seascapes on the wall, the rustic brown balcony outside with its round table and old-fashioned parlor-type ice-cream chairs. We spent much of our time on this balcony, watching the student activity on the campus, talking.

The first day I could tell that my husband had a heavy load of fear on his heart, but he tried not to show it. We began discussing the medical details involved with the valve replacement operation. Heart surgery was always risky, but the doctors had assured John that the percentages were in his favor.

While we were drinking cokes together, John thought back to age nine when he had rheumatic fever. He barely remembered it. It wasn't until five years later that a doctor told him he might have a heart problem some day, but not to worry. When John heard his mother praying one night for his heart to be healed, John began to worry. Then a close friend was killed in a car wreck.

John's eyes had a far-off look. "One day he was there full of life, then my happy joyous friend was gone. I saw death then as a cheater—a robber of life. He was after me, too. Here was my very real enemy. How I hated him. Then you were near death and I was almost paralyzed with fear and anger at my old enemy. When you came back from death to tell me how beautiful it was, you threw me for a real loss."

"It's no loss, John. It's a gain, a plus. You don't have to hate death any more. He can be a friend. I know. Trust me, John."

"I accept your experience, Bets. I believe in heaven. And I would like to feel that death can be a friend. But I love it here so much. I love you and Brenda and my work and the outdoor life. I just can't believe that the next world will be as good. Tell me again what you saw."

Once more I told him the story of my death, remembering

the details as if it had happened yesterday . . . the feelings of joy and lightness . . . the colors of grass, sky, jeweled walls . . . the glorious music . . . then the intoxication and purification of that intense yellow light. "It was a blinding light because I don't think I was supposed to see the Person of Jesus," I mused. "But how I felt His warmth."

"You said you wanted to go inside the city," John continued. "Why? What did you think you'd find there?"

"I wanted very much to go inside because it looked so beautiful and the music was, well, so heavenly."

"But beauty and music are here, too, Bets. Plus so much more. I've always heard that heaven was beautiful with wonderful music. What else did you see?"

"The Person of Jesus. His Presence excited me more than anything I had ever known. I felt I could learn from Him the answers to every question I ever had. I felt that He knew me better than anyone in the world and loved me completely in spite of my faults. It was His love that really got to me. I wanted so much to go inside and be with Him and worship Him."

John's eyes were now shining. He was more relaxed, and I sensed he was beginning to feel some of the intense love of Jesus I had felt.

Early the next morning before John was awake, I slipped out of bed, put on a warm robe, picked up my Bible and crept out on the balcony. The pink rays of the early morning sun filtered through the trees onto the dew-covered Florida campus. As I took deep breaths of the morning freshness, I thought back to John's and my conversation the night before. John's determination to know every detail of my walk with the angel had both stimulated me and made me uneasy. Did he feel he was going to die? He was facing a serious operation, but the doctors were optimistic. No, I concluded, John just yearned to be healed. He wanted his vitality back again.

Yet I needed to provide every possible kind of reassurance for him. I closed my eyes and sought again the Presence. "Jesus, is there anything more you have to tell me?"

The Lord had given me total recall of every phase of my time in heaven, except one. I joyously sang a song which was rendered in many parts and in several different languages by many other voices. At the time I understood the words and thought I would never forget them. Yet later I could not remember either the words or the melody.

As I prayed for an answer to this on my motel balcony, these words flashed before me:

You see through a glass darkly.

Quickly I turned to the well-known thirteenth chapter of First Corinthians on love. Carefully I read it over in my King James Version. With rising excitement I wrote down certain verses and studied them, at the same time keeping up my prayer dialogue.

For now we see through a glass darkly. . . . Our obvious condition in this world, Lord, is not to be able to see or understand the mysteries of the world to come.

But then face to face. You have already shown me that at death we come face to face with you, Lord.

Now I know in part; but then shall I know even as also I am known. We have partial knowledge now which will become full awareness in heaven. This must mean, Lord, that in Your City we will know everyone there, just as everyone there will know us. And in heaven we will have instant knowledge of all the other languages (. . . *we shall be like him, for we shall see him as he is*—I John 3:2).

108

When I stood at Your gate, Lord, I had this knowledge; I knew the meaning of all the different words in all the different languages! But this knowledge was withdrawn once I returned to this world. I suppose it had to be this way, Lord, otherwise having such wisdom in this world would give me an exalted status.

For an hour I prayed and read His Word and was enriched by the bits of knowledge He dropped into my mind and heart. Then John awoke and we sipped coffee and prayed together.

Later that day we were sitting on the balcony watching the shadows of trees and buildings lengthen as the sun sank below the western horizon. John had gone through some heart tests in the morning, then had slept several hours in the afternoon. He was rested, eager to continue his questions.

"Years ago, Bets, the pastor in our church preached that we make our heaven or hell on earth. That made sense to me then. But not now. I've come to believe there is a heaven after this life. I'm just not sure I'm going to like it. I'll miss so many things. Sports, for example."

"What makes you think there'll be no physical activities in heaven?"

"What makes you think there will? I can't imagine playing ball in long flowing robes."

"The Bible says Heaven will be a busy active place."

"I don't know that passage."

It was in the 65th Chapter of Isaiah: *Therefore thus says the Lord God. . . . Behold, I create new heavens and a new earth. . . . They shall build houses and inhabit them; they shall plant vineyards and eat their fruit . . . for like the days of a tree shall the days of my people be, and my chosen shall long enjoy the work of their hands* (Isa. 65:13, 17, 21, 22).

We talked at length about the kinds of work there could be in God's City. John wanted to know other passages which promised life after death. I did some research and came up with the following:

Rejoice that your names are written in heaven (Luke 10:20).

In my father's house are many rooms; if it were not so, would I have told you that I go to prepare a place for you? (John 14:2).

He [God] will swallow up death forever, and the Lord God will wipe away tears from all faces (Isa. 25:8).

To the thief on the cross, Jesus said: Today you will be with me in Paradise (Luke 23:43).

And then there were those tremendous words I saw in block letters: *Whoever lives and believes in me shall never die* (John 11:26).

I could see that John had no real problem accepting the Bible promises. He just could not believe that the next world would be better than this one. What would there be to do?

"I can't point out any more specifics than what the Bible tells us," I replied. "In the singing I heard outside the gate I felt great joy, vitality, creativity, love, happiness, aliveness. It was anything but dull; perhaps peaceful in a way, but not a bland peacefulness. I had a definite feeling that the minute I entered those gates, I would begin a whole

110

new learning process that would completely absorb every ounce of strength I possessed."

John's eyes were fixed on me intently. "I don't think I quite believed you that morning there in the hospital when you said you had been given a glimpse of eternity. I wanted to, but I just couldn't all of a sudden think kindly of something I had hated for so long. I was grateful that you were well again but I just could not believe that dying could be . . . well, good news."

"I'm sure it doesn't seem like good news to people here on earth who lose people they love," I replied. "I love life as much as you do, John. That hasn't changed. But I no longer see death as an end to life; it's the start of a new life. Life on earth is short; eternity is a long, long time. I'm just so grateful that I've been given a glimpse of where I'm going to be in the forever. And every fiber of my being tells me that if you love God and believe His promises, you have absolutely nothing to fear."

John's eyes suddenly filled with tears. I reached out my arms and he held me like he could never let me go.

Later that night we were sitting out on our small balcony again, holding hands and drinking in the sweet aroma of frangipani blooms. John was relaxed and romantically attentive. I confessed to him that I had never felt right about following Dr. Bherne's advice on contraceptives.

John was in quick agreement. "The Lord gave us His word on the subject before we had Brenda. He said He would pour His Spirit upon our seed, and His blessing upon our offspring. How much plainer can that be?"

I felt remorseful. "How wrong we were not to realize that God had an answer to this problem all along," I replied. With my contrition there came the gentle but sudden awareness that He was preparing me again for motherhood.

The tests went smoothly for John and the four days turned out to be the most wonderful period we had ever had together. There was time to talk, to rest, for making love, for prayer, time for absorbing Scripture together, to explore seafood restaurants, time to rediscover how much we cared for each other.

At the end of our second honeymoon, John made the decision to go ahead and have the operation. A date was set for May 12th, two months from then.

Five weeks later I was sitting on a low brick wall, lined with swaying palm trees, at the back of our home in Clearwater. I was having my first cup of coffee and thought to myself, "What a glorious April dawn! Thank You, Lord, for the beauty and fragrance of Your out-of-doors."

I now started each day with Jesus' name on my lips. This morning while meditating I was aware of a strangely sweet sensation. Like the whisper of a wonderful secret, it dawned on me . . . I was expecting!

"Lord, how exciting; but is it all right?" I wondered. Did I have something new to add to the needles of worry in my spirit about John?

It was a fragile moment. The sun was warm on my body. The birds were singing. God seemed to be caressing my troubled spirit, flooding me with His love. I was to depend upon Him for everything and He would be with me. His Spirit would fill me with strength; the healing work in my body was continuing. I was not to worry about the new life in my womb nor think about Dr. Bherne's warning; He would take care of it.

John was very sober when I went with him to the hospital; Mother and Dad were on hand, too, since they had moved to Florida earlier, Dad taking the pastorate of a small church in Palm Harbor nine miles away. Mother and Dad Upchurch were also present. Then the six of us had prayer together in John's room before the operation.

After the surgery the doctor appeared to tell us that all had gone well. His reassurance was premature. The operation was a success, but the surgeon had decided to use a new process of thread-type valve instead of the longer method of suture. The new thread closure let a blood clot slip through, causing paralysis on John's right side.

For days John lay in his hospital bed depressed, wanting to come home. Then through a registered nurse who lived next door, we equipped a bedroom in our home with the medical equipment John would need. The hospital approved our setup, and plans were made to bring him home.

At 9:30 on a Monday morning, Brenda and I arrived at the hospital to engineer the triumphant homecoming. As we entered the room, John was propped up in bed looking toward the door.

Brenda ran to him, "Daddy, you're going home." There was no reply. Something was wrong. John's eyes were open, peaceful, but glazed. Brenda tugged at his robe sleeve, "Daddy, it's really true . . . you get to go home." In a panic, I ran to the nurses' station to get help.

A doctor and a nurse soon rushed into the room with emergency equipment. It was too late. My thirty-six-year-old husband was gone. I was numb, plunged into darkness, only dimly aware of Brenda beside me, sobbing silently.

10

ALL THINGS COME TOGETHER

IT IS HARD for me to understand the blackness that came over me after John's death. I thought I was prepared for this possibility. John and I had been given a beautiful time together at Gainesville where we saw clearly that God had permitted me a glimpse of His City so that I could share it with John.

Instead of acceptance and looking to God for further illumination, I became obsessed by post-mortem what-ifs. What if we hadn't moved to Florida? What if he had gone in for the operation two years earlier as the doctors advised? What if he had had it done at the Miami hospital? What if the doctor had not used the new nylon valve technique? The list went on and on, but nothing changed the medical fact that John had died and the cause of death was ventricular fibrillation.

The time with John's parents at the funeral was devastating. Oscar Upchurch—sad, dignified, courteous, distant. Dorothy Upchurch—grief-stricken, emotional, as always

114

sharp with questions. She never put it into words, but I felt the accusation in her sorrowful dark eyes: "You never believed me, Betty, but I warned you this could happen."

At the grave site Mother Upchurch wept uncontrollably. I felt I could almost read her thoughts. "Why did it have to be Betty who recovered and my John who was taken?"

Brenda was sobbing too, a lovely blonde young beauty with a colt-like appearance, soon to enter her teens. Why did she have to be deprived of a father at such a crucial time in her life?

Gary, beginning to shoot up at twelve, hovered about me in a protective manner. "I'll come stay with you, Sis, and help out around the house," he said, his hand patting my arm just like John was always doing.

The reassurance of my parents and brothers was strengthening, but no one could help me at the point of my greatest need. I felt deserted by the Lord. Let down. Yes—I'll admit it—betrayed. Ever since I had been cleansed and restored in His light, I had felt His Spirit dwelling in me. It had been a glorious, indescribably beautiful period. During the tornado He was there to guide me out of danger; in a hundred small daily crises He had been my rock and strength. But now, an expectant mother, I felt alone, desolate, abandoned, rebellious, angry.

John died on June 15, 1965. For two weeks I carried the grief, going no place, hiding at home. Instead of seeking strength and assurance from the Lord, I remembered the composure of Jackie Kennedy at the funeral of President Kennedy and was determined to put on a duplicate of her act. Pretending to be someone else, of course, never works.

It was Brenda who jolted me out of my self-pity. I had finally left home to go shopping one day at the supermarket. A teenage boy had carried two heavy sacks of groceries to the car for me. When I arrived home Brenda met me at the carport. I was sliding from under the steering wheel holding one of the overloaded bags.

"Mother, you should not lift that much weight. Let me carry it for you," she called.

"Don't fuss over me," I snapped back. "I'll do it myself."

"Mother, let me help. You must think of the baby." She grabbed one side of the sack and tried to pull it from my arms. I resisted.

Brenda suddenly became very stern. "Mother, let go of the sack! I can't carry it for you if you insist upon holding onto the sack!"

The dam broke inside me. Light poured into my mind. I let go, ran into the house, into by bedroom, dropped onto my knees and for the first time since John's death the tears came. For His Word once again flooded my heart, sparked by Brenda's sharp rebuke. There it was in bold letters:

Surely He has borne our griefs and carried our sorrows (Isa. 53:4).

"Oh, Jesus, I will let go of my heavy sack. Forgive me for holding it so tightly that I couldn't hear Your word or feel Your presence. I've let it all go right now, Lord. I am so tired of the burden. Please take it. Please come back to me. Please . . . please, Lord."

When I got up from my knees, the weight of depression was lifted. For the first time I began to see how completely John and I had been prepared for his passing.

Being able to share with John the beauty of death had helped my husband go into the next world unafraid. He would be met and escorted to the King's palace. There would be music which John loved, people he knew, unlimited time and space to be and do all he had ever dreamed about. Greatest of all would be the teaching and fellowship and love of the Lord Himself.

The suddenness of John's passing had temporarily blinded me to the gentle and loving way we had been brought to the moment of his death. Invalidism would have been agony for John, agony for those of us who loved him. God had been merciful. Now I fully understood John's rapt attention to my experience on the other side, his coming back to it again and again. "You say, Betty, that there was such a feeling of vigor and lightness. . . . You really did want to go inside that gate, didn't you?"

Several nights later God completed this healing by sending a special message to me through a dream. I was walking down a dusty path leading to a crude stone shed. I noticed the door was open and walked inside. There an elderly man wearing a cobbler's apron was molding some damp red clay into cups, urns and pots. Behind him on the shelf were pieces of beautifully decorated pottery.

Suddenly a plain jar fell to the floor. The man, paying no attention to me, bent over and picked up the cracked vessel. While holding it gently, he reached into an urn nearby, dipping his fingers into warm molten liquid, and began to seal the broken vessel with the wax. He finished mending it and placed it back on the shelf behind him.

Then he saw me and smiled. "It is better to be a broken vessel, mended and sealed by the Holy Spirit and thus ready to serve, than a vessel without flaw, ornate and beautifully decorated, but unwilling to serve."

I awakened. Any doubts that I could ever be used of God again because of my flaws were gone. Tears of joy and repentance began to flow freely. I felt the warm wax of the

Holy Spirit pour over my wounded spirit in healing power!

The crack that had come into my broken heart had been mended. Once again I had peace and joy in my heart. Everything was right again between me and the Potter. I was ready and eager to be poured out for others in the Lord's service.

Filled with assurance that the block between myself and the Lord had been removed, the next morning I was on my knees determined to bring to His attention some of the unresolved matters that had been on my heart. I had scarcely begun my few words of petition when I felt His gentle correction: *You have always been a controlling woman, Betty. Now stop trying to manipulate Me and listen.*

This quieted me and the Holy Spirit began His teaching: *You have learned, Betty, how pride and resentment can cripple you. You have been freed of your ill feeling toward people like Art Lindsey, your prejudice toward the blacks, your love of material possessions. I cannot answer your prayers now as long as you hold unforgiveness toward your mother-in-law.*

Shortly thereafter I wrote a long letter to Dorothy Upchurch, parts of which I've reconstructed here from memory.

Dear Dorothy:

Ever since John's death I've been wanting to write you a letter and try to say some things that have been on my heart. The Lord is telling me that now is the time; that He wants to do some healing work in our relationship.

First of all, I want to confess that from the beginning of our marriage I felt very jealous of John's closeness to you and I resented the fact that you knew so much and I knew so little. But I was a stubborn and proud woman and felt that I was quite able to run our home, be a loving wife to John and a good mother to Brenda. The Lord has shown me in recent years that I need to depend much more on Him and much less on myself.

I was too grief-stricken to try and talk to you at the time of the funeral. I did not understand why the Lord spared me and took John. Lately I've stopped trying to understand theological issues and am content again to trust that God knows what He is doing. There is the wonderful assurance that John is with the Lord being more fulfilled than he ever was here on earth.

Please forgive me for the resentment I've held against you all these years and for every hurtful thing I've done to you. Since we both loved John so much I do feel the Lord wants us to heal our differences and bring our two families closer together.

Thank you for hearing me out. May God bless you and prosper your family.

With love,

It was several months before Mother Upchurch answered. Then she did, a sweet note. The relationship was restored.

As the seed which John planted in my body during our Gainesville honeymoon grew and developed, I fastened again onto God's promise that He would "bless our offspring" and overrule the gloomy medical prognosis. When John passed away, my faith had wavered. John had ignored the warning of his doctor and the doctor had been right. John had paid the price of living at an accelerated tempo.

Since John and I had gone against the advice of my doctor and I had become pregnant, would the doctor be proven right again? Would I bear a deformed baby?

When the dark cloud lifted, thanks to Brenda's sharpness with me, faith and hope returned. Dad, Mom, Brenda and I began to prepare for a happy blessed event sometime around the middle of December. The four of us began the countdown. "It will be born on Christmas Day—our gift to Jesus on His birthday," predicted my mother.

But in November our doctor began to doubt that it would be a full-term baby. Just before John's death I had nearly suffered a miscarriage. The early pregnancy months had been filled with such tension and hyperactivity that the doctor became increasingly uneasy as the weeks went by.

On November 27 he entered me into the hospital in Dunedin, Florida. Labor began the next day. At 5:28 P.M. on November 28, a five-pound, two-ounce baby girl was born three weeks prematurely. We named her April Dawn because of my awareness early one April morning seven months before that God had created her.

November 28 was also Thanksgiving Day. Again, what a perfect timing He has! And how much we had to be thankful for! April Dawn was as normal and healthy and perfect a baby as this mother, with overflowing heart, could ask.

I can see now that all along God had been preparing me for new life. He did it by bringing me close to death so that I could view firsthand what a joyous experience it was. He restored my body and brought new life out of it in the form of a beautiful baby girl. God will always bring life to every situation.

Why God chose me—a selfish, proud, unloving person— for this unusual experience I'll never know. Perhaps, just as Joshua and Caleb went out to spy the land and brought back the grapes of Eschol (Num. 13:23), God let me spy out the heavenly city so that I could come back and tell everybody how great and beautiful it was. Perhaps he spared me so that I could reassure John that there is no reason to fear death, that he had a glorious adventure ahead of him, that Jesus was waiting to greet him with loving open arms.

AFTERGLOW

THE CALL AWAY from Florida and to a new life in the west began with the death of my gentle and devout mother—Fern Perkins—on December 19, 1969. Several months later, Brenda began seriously thinking of attending a college the following September in Springfield, Missouri. Brenda, April Dawn and I drove to Springfield to look over the school and enroll her, if it seemed right.

It was a low period for me. There was the recent loss of my mother, I had gone through almost five years of the loneliness of widowhood, and now I was having to face up to the fact that Brenda would soon be away at college.

Shortly after arriving in Springfield, we fell in love with and bought an old, three-story, twelve-room Victorian house, a hundred-year-old landmark. The girls and I began immediately restoring and redecorating the interior. We decided to stay on in Springfield, had our furniture and possessions shipped to us, and the girls enrolled in local schools.

At almost the same time we were led to settle in Springfield, one of God's special missionaries, Carl Malz, decided to move his family from Beirut, Lebanon, to Springfield. His wife Wanda was terminally ill with cancer. Connie, their daughter, was thirteen. Carl had been overseas for many years in Egypt, served as President of the Southern Asia Bible College in Bangalore, India, and founded the Middle East Evangelical Theological School in Beirut in 1968.

Wanda Malz died several months after arriving in Springfield.

While teaching a Vacation Bible School class in church that next summer, I was attracted to a young teenage girl who was having trouble adjusting to her new home. Connie Malz and I had a grief we could share together—we had both recently lost our mothers.

It was Connie who introduced me to her father. Carl and I knew almost from the beginning that God had brought us together. Connie confirmed it when she confided to me, "You're the first lady I've met whom I'd like to have for my mother."

April Dawn the previous Christmas had asked, "Oh, God, give me a daddy for Christmas—a big 'un."

Carl Malz is six feet three inches tall and weighs 205 pounds. He and I were married the following June 3, 1971. Several months later Carl received a call to the Trinity Bible Institute in North Dakota to teach Foreign Missions. We were there for four years when Carl accepted a pastorate in Pasadena (outside Houston), Texas, where we now live and work.

Brenda did not enroll at the college in Springfield, but at Presbyterian College, Jamestown, North Dakota. There she fell in love with the son of her professor. She and Miles Millard Smart III were married in July 1974. Everyone calls him Bud. We tell people that "Bud went to college to make Bud-wiser, but Brenda went to college to get smart and did—Bud Smart."

Several years after Mother passed away, Dad moved to Kennard, Texas, a small town 159 miles north of Houston where his son Jim has a cattle ranch. Dad, at seventy, works on the ranch, teaches a Christian growth class at his church and handles a counseling ministry, giving him a full, balanced, rewarding life.

Meanwhile, Mother Upchurch and I continued our correspondence. She and Oscar had retired to a small place near Albany, Kentucky. I'll never forget the visit we made there in August 1976. Brenda and her husband, April Dawn and I flew to the nearest airport and then rented a car to drive the additional 126 miles. Inside, I marveled at how important this visit was to me. When Mother Upchurch lived only a short seven blocks away when John and I were first married, I hardly ever went to visit her; now it was costing us almost a thousand dollars and I could hardly wait to see her and Oscar Upchurch.

It was almost sundown when we drove into the driveway of their small nature farm at the foothills of the Cumberland Mountains in Duvall Valley, Kentucky. From Mother Upchurch's letters I learned that they raised their own food through beef cattle, corn, grain, and a small orchard.

Dad Upchurch was on the porch of their five-room house, standing tall and straight, with hair now white, blue eyes faded, as he greeted us. Tears brimmed his eyes. Mother Upchurch burst forth from the kitchen, dark hair now full of gray, her step slowed, but the vitality still there. She hugged us, one by one. It was real. The love was genuine.

We sat down to a table groaning under home-grown food: a famous Kentucky smoked ham, homemade corn-bread, homemade jelly, applesauce from fresh apples, fresh vegetables, milk, cheese. The next day was spent in talk, leisurely walks about the farm, while the two elderly people feasted their eyes on their two grandchildren. How important it is to keep these family ties, I thought to myself.

Before we left on the third day, Mother Upchurch presented me with several jars of blackberry jelly. Dad Upchurch whispered to me that back in June when his wife knew we were coming, she had climbed the mountain paths in the area, picking wild fresh blackberries and making the jelly the old-fashioned way, slowly boiling the nectar together with sugar for hours until it had the right consistency.

That night back in our home I saw it: Dorothy Upchurch had always been the same sweet thoughtful person I had seen that day. I had simply been too self-centered, jealous and blind to see her as she really was. Why had I not been able to accept people as they were rather than always wanting to change them? Why could I not live fully and joyously in the present moment?

Now I knew! I had to die in order to live.

Joy Cometh in the Morning

O Lord my God, I cried unto thee, and thou hast healed me.

O Lord, thou hast brought up my soul from the grave: thou hast kept me alive, that I should not go down to the pit.

Sing unto the Lord, O ye saints of his, and give thanks at the remembrance of his holiness.

For his anger endureth but a moment; in his favour is life: weeping may endure for a night, but joy cometh in the morning.

And in my prosperity I said, I shall never be moved.

Lord, by thy favour thou hast made my mountain to stand strong: thou didst hide thy face, and I was troubled.

I cried to thee, O Lord; and unto the Lord I made supplication.

What profit is there in my blood, when I go down to the pit? Shall the dust praise thee? shall it declare thy truth?

Hear, O Lord, and have mercy upon me: Lord, be thou my helper.

Thou hast turned for me my mourning into dancing: thou hast put off my sackcloth, and girded me with gladness;

To the end that my glory may sing praise to thee, and not be silent. O Lord my God, I will give thanks unto thee for ever.

(Psalm 30:2–12, KJV)